Among the scenes which are
deeply impressed on my mind, none
exceed in sublimity the primeval
forests undefaced by the hand of man.
No one can stand in these solitudes
unmoved, and not feel that there is
more in man than the mere breath
of his body.

—Charles Darwin

What difference is there between
the human body and the body of a
tree? In truth, there is none: the
consciousness which animates them
is identically the same.

—The Mother,
Sri Aurobindo Ashram

TALKS
with
TREES

by
LESLIE
CABARGA

First Edition

*for Casey
and Anna*

ISBN: 0-9657628-0-7

Library of Congress Catalog Card Number: 97-93558

Edited by Marga Kasper and Diane See.
Designed by Leslie Cabarga
Set in Adobe PALATINO, and Cabarga PROGRESSIV

Printed in India by the Sri Aurobindo Ashram Press
with cover and end papers made by the Ashram.

 ICONOCLASSICS PUBLISHING COMPANY
P. O. Box 48524
Los Angeles, Ca 90048
Tel. 213 549 0700 Fax 213 549 0202

Tel: (323) 549 0700. E-mail: lescab@flashfonts.com

C O N T E N T S

PAGE 139 / CHAPTER FIVE:

To The Redwood Forests

PAGE 165 / CHAPTER SIX:

A message from Mother Earth

LIST OF ILLUSTRATIONS

INTRODUCTION

 *remember the first time I talked to a plant.* I was standing on line at the bank. I glanced over to a small display of live flowers sitting in a shallow pot upon a counter top. "Hi!" I ventured, "How are you?" The plant answered me meekly, which I was to discover is characteristic of plants. "Oh, not very well," it said. "We are trying our best to grow lushly and beautifully for everyone to appreciate, but it is hard under the circumstances." I looked around. Rows of fluorescent lights lined the ceiling. There was no natural illumination. The piped-in air was stagnant. I understood.

The plant repeated its intention to do its best and I was struck both by its selfless resolve to fulfill its function, and the lack of resentment over its situation. This delicate little assortment of flowers was a kamikaze of love, fulfilling its obligation to its creator with every ounce of energy, and oblivion its only reward.

After that, I spoke to some palm trees lining a sidewalk on a quiet street in Hollywood, California. These palms also expressed the desire simply to grow, to look beautiful and perform their jobs as well as they could.

While sitting at a sidewalk cafe in Barcelona one evening, I decided to strike up a casual conversation with a nearby shrub. Lacking a better opener, I asked my usual question, "Hi, how are you?" It answered me annoyedly: "You woke me up!" I'd never thought about it before, but from that experience I learned that a shrub needs its beauty rest too!

Everything has consciousness. Even rocks. Buildings may have some sort of soul. Once, in the middle of the night, the fireplace in my room introduced itself to me as "the spirit of the house nestled in this hearth."

As a child, I learned that plants are conscious beings. I cultivated an avocado pit in a glass of water suspended by toothpicks. It grew well and soon I replanted it in a pot. Then I heard that some people talk to their plants. So I greeted my avocado every day and it thrived. But I wasn't told that plants can answer back. My discovery of this fact came many years later as an unexpected adjunct to my own spiritual replanting.

This awakening came in 1979 when I was introduced to *A Course In Miracles*. In this amazing book, it was explained that one can ask a question and then listen for an answer from a "still, small voice." I have since learned that this "voice" may be that of one's higher self or any of a variety of dead relatives, spirit guides, angels, and even ascended master teachers. I believe that they relish the opportunity to share ideas, offer suggestions and answer our questions whether sacred, profane, or merely mundane.

From the beginning, I repeatedly affirmed my wish to connect my consciousness only with that of loving energies and more highly evolved beings whose wisdom, I hoped, would be profound. So it came as a surprise, when I began interviewing plants, that many of these souls were not necessarily wise, though quite humble and kind; and sometimes with perspectives not much different than yours or mine.

Some readers may wonder how plants—even Spanish ones—can speak English. I suspect that non-verbal concepts received from plants (and other spirits) are impressed upon the framework of our understandings. From there they are spontaneously translated into the language of the receiver; English, in my case.

I once asked my spirit guides how information was conveyed to me. They told me they sent "discrete quanta" of information into my brain. I wasn't familiar with the word *discrete* [a distinct segment]. But when I looked it up, I found that its use was entirely appropriate.

A friend of mine complained that my tree transcripts didn't sound very "tree-like." I wondered if he expected trees to talk like Tarzan ("Me tree, you Leslie."), or like Walt Whitman. I've found that contemporary spirits communicate in a contemporary manner that is not imitative of flowery nineteenth-century poetry.

To me, I am clearly speaking the words my subjects have chosen. Even so, I am constantly amazed at the sentences that I hear, and how they seem to be of a different style or viewpoint than my own. The ideas expressed are so often ones that I feel I'd never have come up with myself that I'm reassured that I'm actually channeling, and not just writing fiction from somewhere deep in my imagination.

For example, once I asked to connect with the spirit of Mahatma Gandhi (and to my delight I began to converse with him). He told me, "I am working now with many leaders to effect peace and also will be coming back again, this time as a worldly pragmatist." I marveled that by myself I'd never have come up with that phrase, "worldly pragmatist."

After I'd begun interviewing plants, I discovered *The Findhorn Garden*, a book about the community which developed many years ago in a rather inhospitable part of Scotland. With nothing but gravelly "soil" to work with, several people, guided by plant devas, or spirits, were instructed to create a garden. Findhorn has since become world famous for its quality, abundance, and diversity—not to mention the miracle of its existence in the first place!

Inspired by Findhorn, I began asking not only the names of certain plants, that is their own "given" names, but that of the devas or spirits who watch over them. I was thereby introduced to Amnel, a rather distraught tulip; Fanwright, one of the spirit captains of Bermuda's agriculture; and to the Great Council of the Redwoods which spoke to me in Marin County's Muir Woods.

In San Francisco, I visited the wonderful Conservatory in Golden Gate Park, a Victorian-era greenhouse where all the plants felt more vital, energetic and happy than any I'd previously encountered. I was told, "The lives here are so happy! It is a blessed place where many can come to feel awe in our presence." Here I met (psychically encountered) Pan, the boss of all plant devas, whose words I would like to share with all of you "budding" plant psychics out there:

I come to all the great places of growth. I am every place at once. It's good to see you making pilgrimages to all the growing spots. You are growing too—perhaps not so green!

When you speak to the heart of a flower or a tree, speak softly. Do not frighten them. They are not aware of you at first. They hear a voice; a question and want to respond, but many don't know how. It takes a while to respond to you. Beware of filling in the spaces [in channeling] so you are talking to them, not to yourself! Wait. Wait for the response to come from the plant. Don't be impatient. Have belief that you are connecting your intention to them as you have to me.

Do you not think yourself important enough to be speaking with Pan? I am everywhere, for it is my duty to take care of all growing things. I have many helpers. Would you like to see us? Start by closing the eyes, using the mind's eye first. This is how it shall begin.

Believe in me. Believe in life, and in the certainty that all is as it needs to be. Believe in the sanctity of the way of Earth and its evolutionary plan. If it should not be this way, it would not be. There must be such expressions as war at this time, even though that upsets you. It is for them to war and you to be upset. This is how it works. Know that life has its trials—life is a trial. Have love for each second, even those without apparent meaning, and even those that don't speak; that are silent. Let this be your celebration of life as it is ours.

I'd like to encourage everyone to begin talking to plants—and listening! Many people, in their prayers and meditations, make inquiries and requests but often stop short of listening for an answer in return. For some, talking with trees may be a stepping stone toward contacting your own spirit guides. With a plant, you can at least see and touch the entity you're speaking with. And few would suspect a plant of being an evil spirit, a common worry of those who begin casting their lines out into the uncharted waters of the spiritual realms.

You may wonder at first if what you hear is only your imagination. Many mediums initially worry about this. Keep trying to listen, but be patient and not too obsessive. Relax, try it on the spur of the moment. As you begin to have success you'll gain confidence. Of course, it is always necessary to evaluate the quality of the response you are getting. If it should seem upsetting or negative, you will want to reaffirm your intention only to communicate with loving energies. This is the key. The strength of our intention extends across the universe to form an impenetrable shield of protection against that which we find undesirable.

For some, talking with trees will take time. Others will have immediate feedback. Know that a sincere desire to talk with spirits is always, eventually, successful. These beings would no more fail to acknowledge you than I would if you greeted me on the street. But whereas I might wonder if you are a kook, your spirit guides already know you intimately and eagerly encourage you to make contact. In a sense, they require your summons before they can come to you because they respect your free will too much to intrude uninvited. Call today! There's no toll charge. Your guides, and plant spirit friends are waiting to hear from you!

Sometimes still, as I sit stroking tree branches and having conversations in my head, I wonder if I'm really making contact with a plant spirit or if I'm just crazy. But what you're about to read is just as I heard it through the grapevine.

—*Leslie Cabarga*

CHAPTER ONE

Close To Home

Sweetgum Tree

"Oh, here comes an old man like me.
See how he walks with a stick? How could I
do that when I *am* a stick?"

*This impressive old tree holds a prominent place in my front
yard. Unfortunately, the sweetgum's prolific output of small, sharply
pointed "fruits" cover the lawn and clog the rain gutters. I spoke with
this affable old gent at the very beginning of spring, before its leaves
had begun to bloom.*

ello. Why don't you like me? Because I throw
my oysters down on top of you? That's
alright. They're my gifts. Yes, there are many
of them. They make some of the animals
happy. That makes *me* happy!

How old am I? About 1927 I was a young pup. I remember
when things were a lot different. The cars didn't drive so fast,
and there were horses too, but not so many. The houses were
the same, but more people were on the street. I was fresh and
strong then, yes indeed. Now I'm old and tired but I don't want

to give up my choice spot. I am happy here. Look, here comes an old man like me. See how he walks with a stick? How could I do that when I *am* a stick [*laughs*].

Oh, it's a warm coat these ivy branches clinging. I like it. They attach to the old, outer part of me. I have many dead parts and I wish you'd prune me because I have to hold them up. It takes energy!

The sun feels warm now. You like it too? It hasn't gotten all the way deep yet. I'm still cool down here. Oh yes, I get out to take a look. That cold, cold weather is what makes me strong. It makes the bark get firm. Yeah, then I've got good strong skin. And the ice makes me pretty when it hangs off. I am away then anyway. I'm deep inside the bottom, in the "basement," all folded up in a warm ball, asleep. You got me from there now. I'm trying to decide what to do next. Should I come out [blossom with leaves] yet or wait? I like to grow. It feels good, but I don't want to get a freezebite. I think I'll wait.

I deliberate like this every year but the truth is, they [the tree spirits] come when it is the right time because, you know, it's not just up to me! There are others who make the rules. They come around to help out, look me over and say "hello." They give me a little holler, then a jab. They say I've got some time left to live. I'm not all done yet. I want to remain for as long as I can.

Yes, others like you have talked to me! There was a lady who used to come by all the time. She'd ask, "Hey there, how are ya doing?" I waited for her, but one day she stopped coming. I think she didn't need to walk this way again.

I think I'm most beautiful in the spring when the new leaves have all finished coming out. Goodbye.

Japanese Maple

> "How can you expect people who are always searching for something outside themselves to ever discover what they truly want?"

It was Fall when I approached this tree, nestled among the overgrown brush that shields the front of my house from the street. Many of its leaves had fallen, and most of the rest had turned a brilliant shade of red. I gently placed my foot on an exposed root and began caressing a branch. This is how I usually introduce myself to plants as I begin to talk to them. Suddenly, the Maple yelled at me disgustedly and, to my embarrassment, I realized I had been caressing a dead branch from another tree which had fallen on top of my intended subject.

 ey, stupid! Yes, that's better [*I removed the dead branch from on top of the maple*]. I suffer much indignity but I am strong indeed. I've been here a long, long time. I don't grow very large. But this is my special place, and I'm proud of it.

Don't you like me?

Sure I like you, except, are you in charge? Why don't you

take better care of this yard? It's not so nice like this. I am a great spirit of the earth. I like things neat, at least to be pruned and loved. But there has been no love here. Not for a long time. There is embarrassment, you see. People here are ashamed and so they don't care about the neighborhood. They trash it. And you are afraid to come out of the house! This is your first time, while all this time I stand, holding my place. See, no other trees are upon this spot. It's mine.

Did you call me 'stupid' before?

Yes. You came close, stepped on my foot, and didn't recognize me because you're not "seeing" with your inner sense, only with your eyes. You're not really looking. Now that I get to address you, I do feel piqued at having been ignored so long by the master of this house and this yard.

Well, it's nice to be appreciated at long last, anyway. But this earth, this air! Let me tell you, it is not happy; like the people. They all want something else. They're here yet they are not here. *[Curiously, I received a greater understanding of the Maple's meaning than its words alone conveyed. I knew that it referred to all the neighbors, walking past everyday, on their way to work, wishing they had better jobs, bigger houses, more money, nicer cars; never living in present experience.]*

I am here. It's my place. I was placed here by loving hands, human hands—if you pick another leaf I'll scream!—Okay, okay, just take one that's fallen already.

Sorry. Why are the lower leaves still green?

The leaves closer to the earth get more moisture and stay green longer.

That sweetgum tree is a nuisance. He's always the center of attention! And look...he's half dead! I'd just like to breathe a little better without these carcasses on me.

You seem to be annoyed.

I am majestic. I feel as you do about this place: no appreciation! But I see it changing. Gardeners may come and make this area beautiful again.

Go then. Have fun. And thanks for opening up this space.

I began hauling the dead branches away from on top of this proud creature. Two maple sprigs had pushed up through the ivy-covered ground. I asked if I should pull them up. "No leave them." the tree said, "They're cute."

Garlic

"When you want to try us, be sure to ask
permission and then we willingly grant it.
Wouldn't you like to be asked first
before being eaten?"

*Ever wonder what an organically grown garlic with green
shoots sprouting from the top would have to say? Let's find out,
shall we?*

es, we are waiting to converse. What do you
want to know from us? We are many from
the one. If we speak as a group, know that
we are still together, in a way that you cannot
know in your life. I perceive you as an individual soul. You have many friends but are not connected or
joined with them as I am with my kin. We speak from the soul
or heart that lives within us all.

What are your special attributes?

You ask what makes me special? You mean besides being
here on your desk? There are no others like me here, I'm sure.

I am the garlic brain. I speak for the garlic seed. You want to know everything, don't you? I can tell you then. Do you like garlic? Do you want to plant us or eat us; fry us up? Either is fine, you know. We await our fate at your loving hands. We don't ask much, nor expect much, but we do not cease our motivation to grow, grow, grow just because somebody places us on a countertop and ignores us. We sprout up and say, "Hey look at us! We're here too!" See? That's how it goes. You can't stop us. Even if you bury us in the ground, we'll start sprouting somewhere, or we'll provide food for the other shoots coming up from everywhere.

You want to know who's in control? Look at your houses and your pavements and your special gardens, all lined up in rows. You like it this way, but there are more of our kind than of your kind. We dominate the scene. We are everywhere. So who really rules this world? You, or the garlic?!

Do you have a special offering to humans in your unique flavor?

We must do what we do according to our own plan. Does this plan include being eaten by humans? Sure, that's part of it. But we exist for our own sake. Watch and see the miracle of our perfection, of the urge of our kind to create our own unique "flavor" in bringing forth the Creator's plan for us. We are simple in form, and our life force is very different from yours, but we are an experiment, if you'd like to call it that, combining our unique contribution with all the other diverse plant styles in the world. We are one more facet of God's ever evolving curiosity: "Let's see what happens if I put this together with this…" He watches us closely. We know we are a small part of the hugeness of all that exists yet we feel important because He placed in us His spark of life and made us grow. This is all we want, really, to prove ourselves by doing what we are made to do.

Do you still live as each clove is plucked off, one by one, and the rest left on the shelf?

How could I not live when now I live still? You are speaking of the transition period. Sure, some part of us could get old and dry up, but there is still this period in which all living things shall leave the umbilical stalk, come to reproductive age, and then to seed.

You enjoy us when we are within this regenerative time in our life-cycles. This is when we are most healthy. And yes, we live, we are alive then. You wouldn't want to eat us otherwise because we wouldn't look very good.

How's my health?

Well, you could use more garlic! There's something that we have to offer, very strong and potent. We are a cleanser. When we come into the body everything else leaves! You may feel we are too strong to be eaten raw, but we are good for the body. Then you'll think we exist just for you humans. We have many functions and for you to enjoy us is indeed one of them. We are a gift to you. We can kill some food poisons and we also make the stomach happy.

When you want to try us, be sure to ask permission and then we most willingly grant it. We say okay to you and your friends who ask first. Wouldn't you like to be asked first before being eaten?

What are your favorite television programs?

This is funny for you to ask, but we cannot "see" television as you can. It does not translate into our consciousness because there is no consciousness in the box. We feel the electrical impulses, but we can only "read" television off of your reactions if we are near to you and concentrating upon you, such as if you were holding us and sending your thoughts to us while viewing.

[Trying to test the garlic's reaction to another absurd question, I asked:] Do you think I should change my hair color?

What is hair? That stuff on top? Why change something? I cannot change anything. Who wants to? Let it be the way it was made to be. You want to put clothes on your hair to make people see something different? Let it be. I told you, eat some garlic and you'll have a healthy body.

What's the last thing you want to tell us?

I enjoyed my life and am still enjoying it although I am a bit wary of the future. If you want to eat me, it's still okay. It's up to you. I am in my protective cocoon, enjoying my growth spurt, my right to everlasting life. If you end it, my spark will move on. That's all. Don't worry about anything. If you want, tell [your readers] we said to eat more garlic for health, then more of us will be grown and that's better! Goodbye.

FOREST CITY
BRAND

POTATOES

Purple Potato

"You should see how the [potatoes] lie about. It is a bliss bordering on orgasmic ecstacy. If you can imagine that going on for a full season you may understand why they are all blissed out and only partially conscious."

People might still be starving in Europe, as our mothers harangued us, *but sometimes you just don't feel like having potatoes, and then it's too late! This organic, purple potato started sprouting so I placed it in water and later interviewed it.*

hat is it? Why do you wake me? I'm growing, coming forth. Will it be possible? It is like a baby soul that knows it's coming into an unwanted situation. There's not much ener-gy invested. I am the same. You don't want me, and you neglected to eat me when the time was right, so I'm expressing myself, my right to flower. I like the water, but it's rather soggy and inhospitable in here. I appreciate the effort, your keeping me on this life-support system you've created. If it means that we shall have this chance to communicate then it has been a good thing. I'm happy to talk, to tell you about myself, but I was sleeping. You must know, you've brought me back from far away, and deep down under for this talk.

You could have spoken to me before I started sprouting too, you know. I was still—my energy was still invested in the body of this potato. I am the small part of this plant's energy split off into this individual form. There is a mass consciousness to which I belong.

I've been told of your progress, your book, and am happy to be a part of it. I want you to know more about what goes on here, where I am. I wouldn't call it a home or a place so much as an awareness of life, of energy, of light. I am "housed" with many others like me. We are all separate, yet together. We are not worried about what to do next for we just know. It all comes out right. Just like you, you never die, neither does a potato, you see. There is always a returning of energy when the form is no longer in its original form. That is, even if we're cut up or eaten or shriveled or squashed.

No, I feel no remorse or sadness about leaving, because I know that the ecstasy of growing will again be ahead for me and my friends. We all look forward to this joy and that is quite a time, you know. It's like just lying in the sun. The sun reaches us as the light energy rushes down through the ground. There is much pulsing, and vibrations which rock us like a cradle, and then everything seems right, seems like bliss. We bask in this time of enjoyment.

Is there a hope for a greater glory? No, hardly. We know of our purpose, there is no striving beyond that. Why should there be, for we know we are fulfilling our God-given mission. But you see, we are very different from you so you cannot think of us as having the feelings or longings you have. I see that you humans are very complex, with energy chains going every which way. Some are blocked or cut off, others extend many places, but you are only aware of a part of yourself as the greater whole [*the higher consciousness*] hovers nearby. You do not see this?

Then me, I am simple, with a simple function: to enjoy growth and then serve myself up to you when the time has come. This I don't mind at all. I am proud to grow strong and really there is such pleasure in it, I cannot tell you. You would say I'm too self-indulgent just enjoying myself so much.

Is there a Purple Potato Deva with whom I could also speak?

The deva you ask of is not here. He is in the field. I can call him and he may come. Don't worry, it's no imposition, I'm sure. He is my friend and will come for me and you. But what I was saying is that if there were no life force within me I would not grow at all, so there has to be a spark of the Creator inside. Yet, it is a different kind than yours. Now here he is.

[Deva:] My friend, I'm glad to be invited to this place, this place so foreign from my soil and the toil that we do there, as we look over our many charges, the many crops under our auspices. What would you have of me today? You want to know first hand how I work? I am the receptor, the intermediary between the love of the One light and the little growing ones beneath me. I care for all of them, and no one is more special than another. I help them grow up good and strong so they may do their work.

You know, there is seldom a bad potato, unless something, such as you humans, gets in the way. We harbor no resentments, for we respect your earthly path and the lessons you are engaged in. We see the outcome as fine; as assured us by the Creator. Therefore, until the time comes when you become clearer and friendlier toward us, and achieve the respect for the plant kingdom, it is still our job to do what we can to make ourselves ready for you by growing and evolving ourselves. Do you not think this so? Do you think you are the only ones who are learning anything and evolving? Nay! We are all coming up together.

At this time I am practicing with new energy fields to accommodate changes in weather patterns, soil growth, and the new breeds of insects coming around. We are also preparing for some earth changes which we are aware of though you may not be because you are not of the earth. There are climate and energy shifts which will alter the current vibrations.

These little potatoes are all my babies. They are really sweet little things and I nourish them and admonish them and prompt them to be strong and persevere. You should see how they lie about. It is a bliss bordering on orgasmic ecstasy. If you can imagine that going on for a full season, you may understand why they are all blissed out and only partially conscious.

We wish your interest were more attached to the soil and in interaction with us on the level that we are present, in the garden proper. We feel some day this shall happen. Until then, when we may meet again, I bid you goodbye.

Apple Tree

It was early Spring when I came around to interview the apple tree in my back yard. For ten years I had not been impressed with this guy. I figured it was some kind of lazy, crab apple tree. Then one season, suddenly and mysteriously: BOOM! I had never seen so many luscious apples. Unfortunately, the interview did not go as well as the fruit production that past year.

h, that time with all the apples was because of the ground water. It just happened that way. It's going to happen again this year. I'd been holding back, you see.

I don't really feel like talking now. Oh yes, I'm coming back for the Spring. Everything is busy now with energy getting ready. That's why I feel tired. This is not a good time.

Red Tulip

"There is a hum or lull in the earth's vibrations that is most restful and beautiful. As a prison, I recommend it."

Every spring, for eleven years, a half dozen pink tulips always sprang up in a corner of my yard. Then one year, three red tulips emerged unexpectedly several feet away from the others. A heavy rain came. Two of the red tulips were destroyed by the force of the downpour leaving one standing alone, its petals miraculously intact. When I interviewed the surviving red tulip my immediate impression was that it was very disturbed. A sense of frantic hysteria struck me. The story of this tulip is unlike any I'd heard before—or since.

 weep for my brothers. We come up only rarely and now they are gone. I am alone. Yes, there are many other plants about—all around me really, yet why do I feel this way? Odd that in this time of regrowth, I feel so fragile, frightened.

I think you're beautiful.

Thank you. It's just that I was with my friends, they were a part of me and now they lie scattered. I feel their pulsing even in the strewn petals. I feel that I'm in a battle zone.

It is sad, really, that something like us of such delicacy must also be so fragile. Yes, I understand the ongoingness of life and that I'll return again. But for my spirit entrapment in this dwelling, it has been…[*The tulip hesitated. Then, referring to a large dead branch nearby:*] He doesn't speak anymore. I will soon be like he is, but my physical frame is so much less. I rot easier. Yes, already I look old though I have been here so briefly. I anticipate greatly my rebirth for it seems boring to be locked in this bulb for so long. My birth time, my alive flowering time is my favorite.

What did you mean by 'spirit entrapment?'

I am a being from another galaxy. Amnel is my name. The others, the Greaters (they sure are great, I mustn't blame them) have placed me here. This entrapment, it's like jail or being sent to a heavenly purgatory. I am, yet I am not. You see what I mean? I am not so enthralled with this life as the other [plants].

My spirit is infinite like yours. I come of many varied experiences, like you. You could just say I am here for now while I pay my dues. It is an ironic sentence, so to speak. On my planet I was young and rash. I acted too strongly, without thinking. It resulted in harm to others. There was a tribunal, and the result was I was placed into this "cell" where I might reflect for a long spell. I am red because of my fervor and I smell sweet because really I am beautiful at heart. Yes, I have a heart as you do.

Having my friends leave while I survived was to be my introduction to the pain I caused the survivors of my actions against their loved ones, do you see? I am feeling quite alone now because I knew [the other tulips] well—we got to know one another well. When I "die" from this flower, it is quite a thing: a withering, diminishing. I retreat down the stem and just go back into hiding for my next brief journey out. I guess I'm still learning. They will call for me when I am to be reintroduced into society again. You could pick me. I'd thrive awhile—at least as long as in this hostile environment. I'd do it for you, to be near you.

Oh, you're writing a book—like a reporter? Tell them I am in a pleasant enough experience. It's only that my longing for my mother and my past friends makes it seem unpleasant here.

Really, there is a hum or lull in the earth's vibrations that is most restful and beautiful. As a prison I recommend it. As for my friends—the dead ones—their violent ends have caused them to finish their sentences. They're going back. There'll be a period of interim confinement—like probation—then they'll get to go back See, I know about this [probation] because I am coming through your field of focus, so I see what you know and can identify conceptually with you.

We are much smaller than you. Yet, where I lived is a bustling cosmopolitan area. Stop, you're making me sad. I had been waiting for you for I knew you were coming. I feel calmed by your love, your attention. Thank you for the time. I will carry you in my heart and visit with you again from time to time.

A postscript: the following Spring only the usual pink tulips bloomed. Neither Amnel, nor his two crimson friends reappeared.

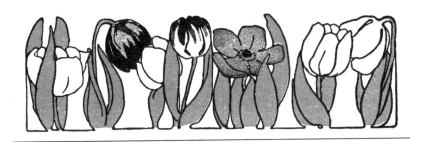

ONION
WHITE GLOBE

LAGO BRAND F. LAGOMARSINO & SONS

Sprouted Onion

"There is a part of me where there
is a light emerging, growing brighter.
The same light exists in all things."

An onion started to sprout while I was on a fast and couldn't eat it. When we spoke, it sounded confused, upset, uncertain. The voice was at once immature yet mature as if the consciousness vacillated between the present incarnation and the higher knowledge of its inner being.

Hello. What can you tell me?

grow, you know. I am coming forth in joy. It feels strange to grow as I do, I'm not sure what is going to happen. I feel that I am not in an appropriate environment to continue so I feel that I shall waste away after a point. Is this true? Oh, I would love it if you were to put me in soil, so I could continue to come forth. But I feel your hesitation. To you I am just a nuisance. Yes, perhaps at the moment you are lovingly holding me but this won't last and I'll be sitting there again on the shelf, to die. Can't I go outside?

Why is it you have so little life in you that you don't feel for me and the others who are coming forth? That's just it, you say you have other things to do. This is my only thing to do. I am coming out. I wish to grow strong and big, to have space and fresh air, but don't know if I'll get the chance now. Yes, I'm soft and beautiful because I am expressing the urge for life. I just want it to continue.

There is a small part of me where there is a light emerging, growing brighter. The same light exists in all things, and from this do I arise. I am not a very bright light or energy because of my doubts. Were I to be a part of a natural environment for growth, one in which I was in communion with other lights, I think I would feel better than being on these hard surfaces. There will come a time when I have nowhere else to go, nowhere to grow into, because my house will be consumed. Then it's all over for me. I am cozy in here for now. It's like your womb, no?

I am part of the larger consciousness, I am not just a little onion plant, no! I know all there is to know. I am just in here waiting for the time when I shall express myself. I told you, I'm cantankerous because I'm trapped. Yet when you don't ask me questions and I just sit here, I'm not so sad because I don't think about sadness. I just think about living and existing. There is a strength I feel as life and growth pulsate outward from the light. It is a rhythmic pulsing that feels rather good, so I can relax in this and feel fine, just enjoying the rhythms and relaxing.

My concentration shifted for a moment. I looked idly around the room, then back at the onion propped up in front of my keyboard. I began wondering to myself what a cross section would look like if I were to cut it in two pieces. The onion read my thoughts, jarring my focus back to our communication as it screamed...

No! Don't open me up! I would be exposed, I would die. You would see the little me inside. I don't wish that. Just to bear fruit and keep going is my meaning. I don't have the other sensory expressions as you do. I only feel the pulsing of the growth and the happiness that comes back to me from my outer limbs as they extend into the light. I send out the light and they bring it back to me and this feels good and it makes me want to grow some more.

I'd rather be free to go outside this...cocoon, to swim free because I did it before. But, I guess I'll just stay here now. So thank you, and I trust you will respect me, as I do you.

Wheatgrass

"Whenever someone takes earth,
which is fallow, and places upon it seedlings,
and nourishes them, we are joyful."

A rush of energy and mental clarity seems to follow the drinking of sweet-tasting, cleansing wheatgrass juice. But at one buck an ounce I decided to try growing some wheatgrass myself. I had never sprouted anything before. After a slow start my blades of grass began to come forth strongly. A few weeks later, I talked to my children.

You don't mind my eating you?

o sir. We are like vegetables. We understand our function. It pleases us to nourish a higher life form and to partake in the nourishing of one who extends our joy into greater areas of exploration. We sit here and it is our pleasure to attempt to grow as best we can for you. We thank you for instigating our lives.

Whenever someone takes earth, which is fallow, and places upon it seedlings and nourishes them, we are joyful. There is a special gratitude; a special grace bestowed upon those with the so-called green thumb—those who give life, like the Mother herself. For as extensions of the Creator, you are giving life by your own hand. Despite your mistakes, and lack of familiarity with the growing process, we yet endeavor to please you, and to grow for you. It is a demonstration of our joy and survival instincts; our yearning to come forth and to grow strong.

You have given us the opportunity to express ourselves in this manner as the Creator has given life to you, and we are full of gratitude, even as you clip us for your own use. And you will find a vying among the members of our group for the opportunity to serve. When a portion is cut there is a shock to the system, but the rest of us pitch in to lend our humming vibration, our tones to help re-set the fractured tone of the ones who have been chopped. And then we continue to come forth. To grow strong for you, and to feed you in your task of enlightenment.

Are you special in the healthful properties you possess?

You want to know if we are a special breed? You would be surprised to know how many varieties of helpful plants and growing things there are if you would but partake. We don't consider ourselves of special merit. We would say that those who survive by instinct alone let nature's sensibility lead them to the nourishment most beneficial to them. You humans are far away from such understandings. Although you do have your cravings, they are often artificial ones arising from the body's addictions. That is, your longings come not from the essence but through the emotional lacks, spaces, holes which entreat, which beg of the physical being for sustenance. And it is true that the physical body is subject to wantings and tastes which are not compatible with the needs of the nature of the being.

Domesticated animals will also become out of touch in situations where their own natural instincts for survival, for the foods which they need to ingest, become distorted or realigned through the ingestion of the humans' prepared foods. Then their whole bodies become altered and their taste buds become changed, realigned.

We began by telling you that many of the grasses, plants and weeds, which you see all around you, are edible. In times past, there were many more people who could divine the beauty and the value in the various buds and bulbs and sprouts that came forth. This is still the case as many adhere to the ancient principles and more are again learning to do so. The drug companies use these same plants, for this is the beginning of it all. These companies extract essences from nature and then try to mask or hide them; to alter them beyond recognition. Do not blame them for they are doing the best they know how within a structure that creates competition and demands progress and profit.

Wheatgrass, how do you feel being in these trays and what could be given to you to make you continue to flourish?

We are happy to have been given life and to be nurtured by you. We belong to you. Our dream would be to spread out and grow more abundantly. However, we are thankful for this experiment in which you have placed us with great concern for our well-being, though not always understanding our needs. We feel your concern and your love, your thankfulness, and appreciation. This encourages us, feeds us. You will know when enough is enough. We will continue to grow and provide you with the nourishment you require. We are toughly rooted, well matted. We lock our arms, our roots and do not worry. Thank you again for your patience with us and your appreciation.

Lettuce

"I am part of a great consciousness of roots, so to speak, connecting all who link together through the soil."

This slim head of organic lettuce from my food co-op came with the rootball intact. The sign described it as recently picked, "living lettuce" so I thought I might be able to speak to it. To my delight, a great session ensued.

ello, I'm ready to talk and have been so. I am feeling melancholy, or was until you arrived, because I like your spirit and recognize in you one who, like me, has done much shedding of outer leaves. The newly opened you is a delight to be around.

You noticed this?

Who wouldn't recognize this new part of you? Well, if you don't recognize it yourself that's because you are still surrounded by the old stuff, the same old feelings and patterns which haven't entirely given way yet. This is just beginning for

you as there has been an opening up of blockages. Good work.

Now I want to talk about you, not me.

We're just telling you why it feels good to be with you. I come from a farm, a small place where they are just beginning to experiment with growing produce for market. Two people to whom it occurred recently that there was money to be made through this endeavor, but who hadn't realized the amount of work involved. We are happy though to be working with them and we are coming around more as we see what's happening.

There is some tension though between them. This turns us off you might say, so we are growing rather tentatively prior to seeing what will happen. The "bad vibes" which sometimes go on have been defeating. Yet we are providing some positive growth to encourage them. There is a delicate balance which must be maintained for us to grow.

Sure, sometimes we grow in the wild, unattended. In such a situation, where we are unencumbered by human involvement, we will often grow exceedingly well. There is often a kind of emotional pollution of the energy waves from humans (which is why we lauded you). Yet, we are *useful* vegetation. Our duty is to feed, and so if there is no use for us we may become discouraged. Oh yes, we have such classifications as "useful."

But don't most plants have a use in food, medicines or fragrances?

Yes, that's true. But some especially display beauty with colors and special fragrances. We call them the "pomp gardenias," for they arrive with that special function of beautifying the place. We're not feeling inferior, no sir. We have our special duty of which we are proud. Feeding, after all, is quite necessary and we see to it, along with the rest of our group, that feeding can occur with great variety. For you know, a variety [of plant species] is necessary to suit the needs of the many people and animals on this planet.

What of animals whose diets consist of but one thing?

A cow doesn't have the emotional or mental complexity, as humans have, which causes different states within the body. Now, these states are good. They are necessary for your growth and development, so that's why a varied diet provides the necessary nutrients and nutritional accents to suit the particular needs of the individual.

How can one half-dead head of lettuce be so knowledgeable?

We didn't say we were only speaking from one head of lettuce, now did we? No! You have the whole garden here with you. That's who we are! We have entered this bunch of leaves in answer to your previously stated idea to serve us.

What do you mean by "serve?"

Serving us is honoring us with your interest, your inquiries and your earnestness, as well as your gentleness and respect for us. We sense that you revere our life energy (as we do yours) and that's what impressed us; that you were afraid of hurting us and so handled us gently.

The healing we bring you comes from the nutrients we offer: just that particular kind that comes from this species. You will know when to eat lettuce or another product. Unfortunately, your taste is not so easily satisfied with what your body really needs for there are other influences—you humans don't trust your bodies to know what they need.

Let's talk more about you. How did you feel when you were picked this morning?

I knew that was to be my fate. I had watched it happen to others and so was not surprised. I was gently wrapped, and I had reached the end of my growth cycle so it was time—there is a time for everything, you know. Now, as I've said, I'm happy to know you, and to inform you of what I know, and to spread my consciousness, overlapping on yours. It's been wonderful to feel you through me! I am part of a great consciousness of roots, so to speak, connecting all who link together through the soil. We are a large and friendly family.

We are all pals, if you know what I mean, even with species of different purposes, like trees which serve neither food, nor beauty functions specifically but have another purpose, perhaps like a horse whose job it is to bear structural burdens and serve mankind in this way.

Yes, as you've been thinking, we are all multi-faceted, serving many different functions at once, none exclusively. A tree can be beautiful. Yes, of course. But for us there are different categories, understand? It might be like you and your varied races of humans, or like a cat compared with a lion, or tiger.

Do you ever worry about the fate of the earth with pesticides and other environmental destruction facing us?

That is not specifically my job. My job entails the here and now, doing the best I can with what I have to work with. Certainly, I sense the strains going on and can experience some deficits in soil, water and air content. Yet my ability is to wring out the necessary ingredients that I require. I can always do this. At least, so far I have been able to. So then my only concern is tasting good and looking fresh for you. I appreciate you. Thank you for letting me speak. Good day.

A postscript: after this interview, I called my food co-op and asked the purchaser about the source of the lettuce. She confirmed that there had been some problems between the grower and his assistant—just as the lettuce had indicated!

302

No. 302

INDIA RUBBER TAPPING

Rubber Plant

"When we die you say it is for lack of water, but we have failed to create an adequate context, either through a misfocus of energy, or a lack of will."

For many years this rubber plant and I shared the second floor studio in my Victorian house. When I got around to interviewing it, I found it had shared much more with me than I had realized.

y name is Arthenparis: *he who waits*. We await resolution. We combine yearnings of energy and spirit to await results. We are with you when you sleep, watching and waiting to see how this unfolds for you.

I experience with you the joys and frustrations of your life though mine is a life merely of being and growing, greeting a new day, growing up strong and experiencing regrowth as my older leaves dry up and fall.

I love it when you stroke me for you have a nice touch and do so with such reverence it makes me love you the more. I ask nothing of you save the incidental watering which I always remind you of. If you can wash off my leaves I'd like that too but will do fine as is. There is no aspiration in my existence other than to grow tall and be happy. I express this through my new growth of beautiful leaves. It is just a natural thing when the old ones fall; they had their day but our goodbye is tempered by the joy of fulfilling once again the promise of life through the optimism of new leaves which reach out eagerly toward the sun.

What do you think of the computer radiation since I got this electro-magnetic field reducing gizmo?

There has been a considerable lightening up of the environment, but if you thought we couldn't handle it you were wrong. This is our task: to take naughty, wild wavelengths and eat them, then spit them out benign. We draw the negative energies toward us and transmute them for you. This is our job. You think photosynthesis is just oxygen exchange? Wrong. It is more a cleansing of the vibratory impulses that accompany, or are part of, the exhalations, the carbon dioxide. We cleanse the stuff. This is why when our leaves, the receptors, are dirty, they are less functional. You see, it is in your best interest to wash me.

Who are you? Are you more than just a rubber plant?

I was wondering if you'd ask that. I am someone who is a

watcher, watching after you, assigned to you. It has been partially through my impetus that you have begun these tree channeling activities. You started feeling my presence and it drew this out of you. It reminded you, actually, of that time as a youth when you were very close to your avocado plant.

Your turning to and from plants at different stages of your life has related to your opening up to yourself—and closing in—at different times. Then we have ridden with you through these past years and have missed you when you've been "away," both literally and figuratively.

I am your gatekeeper to the plant kingdom, my friend. I know much, I am connected you might say, with all plant life. I am but a way station, erected or established in this spot. For you might think this is something silly that you are doing in talking to trees, whereas we feel it is most important. Through your work many others will begin communicating with us, and they will find therein a connection with spirit that in some ways shall become more immediate for them than in tuning in to their own guides. They will find it easier and more acceptable to tune into us. So you see, you are a catalyst in this activity.

How do you feel about not being outdoors in the open air?

I wish most to keep growing, to have the space to do so and

to please those who see and feel me. I am most happy. Although I long to be outdoors to experience the sun first hand, I appreciate the protection from the harsher climate of winter. I can survive winter, you know, and don't mind being outside a pot. I like the environment of your room. I'd like to be closer to you, but in the window I get a taste of the seasonal changes.

You have already learned that a plant's life, as a human's, revolves around necessity, a shaping of function to environment and vice versa, so that without a context, a life of any sort has no purpose. Then, given the context of a pot in someone's home or a spot in a forest, or a trainer pot in a nursery; each of these creates context.

When you ask if a tree makes a sound when it falls in a forest where no one is within hearing, we say no. It does not even exist, save for the context which surrounds its existence. Not that it cannot exist for itself. But you see, even you are not existing save for your projecting of your purpose or your striving onto a physical tangent point somewhere in the universe. If not for an agreement to exist and a framework to exist in, you would not.

We plants will survive in any location if we want to, if we are serving a purpose. When we die, you say it is for lack of water, but we have died because we failed to create an adequate context, either through a misfocus of energy or a change of mind, a lack of will. We may at times attract ourselves to someone who cares not for us and so neglects us. We may commit suicide in this fashion for we derive benefit from coming and going within our own reincarnational cycles. It's that simple.

Do trees and plants enjoy having wind rush through you?

Yes, such stimulus is exciting and encouraging, but you know, in terrible storms we are unnerved as you would be standing there facing off these squalls. Who survives and who doesn't? Would you like to know? There are those whose will provides that they remain while others would just as soon snap in half and move on, spiritually that is.

Do you feel pain?

Pain is hard to describe. It is an interruption in the regular flow of our energy patterns. So if we have become used to the smooth flow and that is suddenly interrupted, the fracture is perceptible. It takes some time for us to come back into alignment, basically to create new flow-around pathways. As soon as this happens we are back to normal again. We like things to be smooth, and we strive for the perfection of our paths and our energetic bodies. When all goes well and perfect; when we grow unhindered, it is best and we are happy. Otherwise, we continue as best we can. Pain...it's more akin to horror at the shock of being interrupted. We've described to you the humming resonance, the continual pleasure-producing rhythm of our growth. All we do really, is respond to nature's impulses and our inner programming. When that course is altered, there may be outrage, or shock.

Let's say you were walking down the street and all of a sudden you bumped smack into a large pane of glass that you hadn't seen. You'd be smarting as well as outraged. Then you'd get up and walk around it and continue your way on your path. Next time, you'd know it was there, and if someone were to trace your footsteps—if you were walking through red paint, say—each time you went back and forth around the obstacle, it would be as if you were creating another ring of growth. But you would not feel the pain anymore. That's how it is when someone nails into us. We get over it! If someone shakes us, it does shock us, because we were going about our business in silence, and peacefulness. So it is a shock, but we are designed to stand it.

Now what happens if someone picks a vegetable off our stalks to eat? There is acceptance of this. After all, why would we have grown so lusciously, except to be eaten? Those born into such a fate are perhaps more willingly resigned to it than you plant lovers might imagine. There is even pride and joy in being accepted for the eating. It means we've done our job correctly.

What do you see in the future regarding earth movements?

You all are so concerned about earthquakes for you like things to remain stable, reliable. Now you have heard many predictions of earth movements coming to get you. There will certainly be upheavals, and these shall alter people's lives in much the same way that wars create disturbances in complacency, causing people to have to realign themselves and learn and grow. Often the growing is not pleasant at all. This, when seen from a higher light, is just part of nature.

We wish we could impart to you an understanding of the way all existence is really designed. If so, you'd see an interconnected gridwork of light energy. You'd see something akin to the way bacteria looks under a microscope. At this level, all life would appear as nothing more than light energy.

Then you'd see the movement, the interactions, even certain parasitic elements overtaking others, but you'd also see that as one element devours another, it simply returns out the back way or, in other words, it creates new patterns of light, so there is never a true devastation. And you'd also see—if you could watch this thing over millions of years—how it evolves, changing shapes and changing patterns.

This is most interesting now, as different rhythms play out. Imagine a cosmic chess game of such mind-boggling complexity that no computer could plot it! And yet there *is* a computer of sorts plotting it. There are those of such intellectual capacity as to make your intelligence seem less than that of worms. No, a thousand times less than worms.

Okay, I'll let you go. Please check back from time to time. There is much to speak of on other subjects.

Another Lettuce

"It's curious to be alive and pulsing with energy, but the one near you, tending you, seems to ignore this, thinking you are like a stone, or dirt."

One month after my first lettuce interview, I sought the world view of another head. From the refrigerated case at my food co-op, I brought it home and placed it in a bowl of water on the window sill. The lettuce regained its full vitality, spreading its leaves wide as though it were growing in a field.

hank you for reviving me. Oh, I know what lies in store for me, but that deep, cold sleep was sad. At least now I have more meaning in my life, thanks to you. I don't mind being eaten by you, I'm bred for this. I am going to enjoy my reward in nourishing you. It is all part of my plan.

How do you feel about having been uprooted, then transplanted by me in this bowl of water?

You could say my soul left my body during this period so that I didn't have to feel the shock of it. I was able to rise up and watch the scene without feeling it as far as the physical sensations involved. I am a joyful creature. I only know this state. For me to be here speaking with you adds to my joy.

Why don't others talk to us as you do? They could, you know. It is interesting for me to be in the same place as somebody who acts as if we are not together, ignoring me. I don't need much attention, I just want to say that it's curious to be alive and pulsing with energy, but the one near you, tending you, seems to ignore this, thinking you are like a stone, or dirt. They do not know we all live—and live together! It is not merely a matter of tending the soil, watering the "plants" and weeding. You wouldn't just feed the baby then leave it alone in the crib until the next day.

We wish that some kind of transference of energy could occur between you people and us similar to that which we plants experience between ourselves. Like when you go to another country, you try to embrace the local customs. When you are in the garden you are in *our* country, see?

What form would this greeting between humans and plants take?

We would like you to stand before us in the silence we share, and feel our energy, smell our fragrance, BE with us in the experience of just being. What would you expect from us whose primary activity is just being and growing; glorying in survival?

This is the way we plants also commune with one another. There's a hum, a pulse you've heard about. We sing together, though not with true sounds, but with the vibrations of our energy, and when we are all growing together, in the same place or garden, we hit a sync and our movements become one and then the energy flows and we may start up quite a song!

When humans are about, we don't often do this, getting to this level that is, unless the people are attuned to us and are not doing disruptive things like uprooting us, or pushing us around. Also, they would need to be in harmony themselves, as arguments or angry dispositions would upset us.

Describe the ideal environment that would allow you to thrive. What can we suggest to farmers?

I would like to be where the warm sun hits me directly, not through a curtain or window, not in a hot room—although that works too—and I'd like the soil to be turned often, mixed with compost, some nice little worms rolling around in there, keeping everything aerated. Moreover, I'd like the planter to come by and encourage me, to touch me, to spend just a little time each day with me and the rest of us sharing the garden. The planter should not just be doing work, but enjoy being with us, in the language of our enjoyment, by opening up to experiencing our energies. And what's more, by allowing us to enter your consciousness we may dwell there for a time. This is sharing, and such cooperation between us produces much happiness and thus bigger crops.

Yes, bigger means better! The happier we are the larger we wish to become to drink in the utter pleasure of being alive and expressing ourselves for you. There is the tendency, you know, to pull up a crop at a certain point to get it to market, and to maintain an equal-looking size of crop. And yet, when the harmony is right between all of us happy crops, we will indeed produce equal sized "specimens."

Oh, there is something so beautiful about plants, all of us, growing together in a field, in the sun, with all the happy little critters, the bugs and worms doing their jobs. If you humans could live like us, think of the cooperation!

You have extended our life for this wonderful interaction, and we bless you for it and hope that we will be a most delicious part of your diet! Thank you!

Hickory Tree

"Peacefulness is my essence.
Nature takes the burden and responsibility.
Let her fret and worry!"

In the back yard of my 1886 Victorian house stands this large and stately Hickory tree. Here is what it had to tell me about the life and times of my home's original owners.

 feel old. I am a house. I give house to many ants and plants. They live on me. It's okay (laughs), it's my job. I've been here a long, long time, you know. I saw many things. Many parties, many dogs, many people and different clothes; very different than now. You should see what I mean. The old people, they were different. I mean their energy patterns were different. More lined up and confined than yours. Your energy is crazy: all everywhere. I can see it. That's okay too. It's better, I think; more free.

I think the old man who owned this house was only happy when everything was as he liked it to be. If he looked out and the lawn wasn't trimmed he didn't like it much. He thought he was a lawn. Keep him and it all trimmed. It was much the same.

Someone once carved something on me but it broke off. I didn't care. It was just a kid playing with a new knife. But, oh yes, the children climbed up. High too. And (laughs) the mother said, "You kids get on down from there!" I laughed because I wasn't going to let them fall. You know, sometimes there are beings who'll push you off a tree. Oh yes! You have to be careful because these sprites are all over the place.

No, I'm not a sprite but I am an old tree, a friend to all the little ones be they human or bug. I love them all.

Have you ever been unhappy?

Yes, when the first owners were leaving it was a time of sadness and change. One died and then the other. Then for awhile nobody cropped the lawn. I had a crisis then. Should I stay or go? A tree can go [extract its soul] you know. You can get permission to leave. Then the tree goes on without its inner life for awhile but then fades away. So I wanted to move on too. But they said to stay. I'm not sure, but either way it's turned out okay.

So you're moving on, away from this home? Well, it's your

time. This place doesn't want you now because you don't want it. It's as simple as that.

What is the essence of you?

Peacefulness is my essence. Not caring to worry. I don't need a thing. I like to feel different energies, weather, people, etc. but I am best just as I am. Nature takes the burden and responsibility. Let her fret and worry! Today and everyday I'm just this. Bless you! Come back again. Wherever you go, nature will take care of you just as she does me.

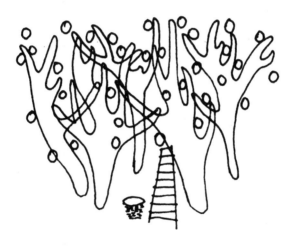

Chrysanthemums

"Give unconditionally, offering of yourself, knowing that there is nothing to lose...you are never in short supply of anything you give out."

These cut mums were a gift to me. I placed them in a vase with water, and later interviewed them. It is convenient when I can bring my interview subjects to me, in front of my computer, rather than repeating their words into a tape recorder and later transcribing. In this case, however, the Mums complained about being so near to the radiations emanating from the computer.

he intensity in this space is overwhelming. Moving us to the side is better, thank you.

You smell lovely!

We smell nice to you? Thanks. It is not as much as before when we grew in the earth, and now we are in a transitional state. We are on the way out, you know. We are happy to be here as a gift to you. This has given us a new mission, especially when we were told that we'd be conversing with you. Few feel the power of us or guess at our depth. The power of our energetic influence and radiating beauty goes far beyond the stems and petals that you can see.

We call out with our fragrance to others, to the bees, to people passing by and we sing a song throughout the day, calling forth more of the same kind of beatific energies who are attracted and attractive to us.

So, you've been thinking about this, no? Of your attractiveness to the humans of your species? Then just like us, put out your fragrance and your energy. Just make sure it is welcoming and attractive. We send out only love energy and ask for nothing; the gifts we bring are our only reward. This is the way we look at it, for we already have everything we need. Didn't we end up here with you? Won't we shortly be returning to our maker for more periods of lovely, relaxing growth in the sun? Everything is all quite well and good then.

Give unconditionally, offering of yourself, knowing that you cannot lose, because there is only more where that came from. You are never in short supply of anything you give out. Yes, it should come back to you in this way. For us we need nothing but have everything. Oh look at that sun coming through. What a lovely day again, eh?

Are you afraid of the cold? Maybe because you must wear coverings and are not adapted to your earth as we are. We are always dressed (laughs). You live far from this soil. You don't know your feet on it and so must fear nature's elements. This is a pity, you know. We rise and fall, live and die as required, and there is nothing more than this cycle of transcendence each time in which we know no doctrine of fear. We have actually experienced the bliss of separation from the physical many times, it is fresh in our awareness, and so there is nothing fearful in it.

Your words are so wise, how do I know it's really you talking to me?

We think you know. Of course, since you speak to invisible entities all the time, how could you be sure? We will say that we are proud to be here with you enjoying the day. We are always glad to converse, so long as we are able. It is not very complicated to be us. We KNOW what is true because we experience it. It is not our purpose, this time, to have such a complex emotional nervous system as yours. We make a simpler job of it. We speak of what we know or what we can see within your knowing. We have no complaints. There are things we might suggest regarding better ways in which we may be cultivated, or about soil conditions. We could speak of rough handling, the lack of love prevailing in the vibrational energy around us, or the situation in the world as we experience it.

The energy from this world that strikes us, that flows through us, is not a peaceful energy. Rather it's a fearful, unsettled, anxious energy. But it is not our place to complain or even suggest. Who would listen? We only know that by doing what we've come to do, and doing it the best we can, we have fulfilled our responsibility. It would remove the conditions of unrest or unhappiness if all did their best and accepted things as they are, which is pretty good—nay, *perfect*—under the sun.

CHAPTER TWO

Ibiza, Bali and Bermuda

Bougainvillaea

"We think the gardener here is inept, snipping roughly at us. We would like to fall on that gardener!"

This shrub was one of my first interview subjects. It was off the coast of Spain, on the island of Ibiza, that I met this brilliantly colored bush. Its beautiful, magenta flowers grow in a most unusual arrangement. The Bougainvillaea became my friend as its blossoms spilled over onto the patio of my hotel room overlooking the Mediterranean. Yes, it's a hard life, that of an itinerant shrub psychic.

 e are friends growing together from the earth, entwined in love and friendship. We are a family, so to speak, growing together, loving together. There is no disharmony but a natural order where we playfully wrestle for the higher growth and better spot. We are beautiful, no? We love all the appreciation we get and this is why we have grown lushly for you and all the others who come and go and admire us. We are showoffs—it is our gift to all of you.

We don't care much for the cold. Though we internalize our juices that are the life of us, to sleep during this time, it is our preference to glow brightly, flowering for all to see. We love ourselves for we are able to be lovely. We think the gardener here is inept, snipping roughly at us. We sadly say goodbye to our lost limbs but feel we are yet complete. Now, who we are is that which we remain, and we embrace this present totality. Also, he sprays those chemicals and we have to turn away in dislike. It is hardly necessary! We would like to fall on that gardener!

There are some animals [bugs] that pick on us, eating the leaves and flowers of us and we don't like this because it hurts, yet we reconcile it because we have perpetuated life through other creatures. We are perennial and come again every year to new faces, to new experiences. Whatever shall come, we are excited to enjoy. We are not that old—only a few years, but we grow fast. It is an expression of our overwhelming urge to love. We know someday we will falter, and this is okay. That's how it should be, for then another will take our place. And if we should provide the seed for this, it will be all the better.

JASMIN

Jasmine Tree

"The spirits of cut flowers often linger if they feel they might enjoy the experience of being among a new group of flowers, and of pleasing people."

This Jasmine tree stood at the entrance of a small hotel at Lovina Beach in the north of Bali. Every morning my friends and I would gather up a few of the beautiful, yellow-tipped, sweet-smelling blossoms that naturally fall off the tree and sniff them during the day.

 am very happy, sir, that you want to sit here with me as I am happy when others come near. Oh it is very interesting for me to be here. I think many forest trees never get to mingle with people and learn about them. Oh the stories of you travelers! I don't understand the details, but I enjoy the laughter, the excitement, adventure, and all the emotion that I pick up on.

Your leaves are so soft and fuzzy.

We are newly growing at all times—always a new sprout or shoot—we draw water up from the ground and grow and grow.

I am about thirteen years old—thirteen seasons, much rain. Oh, the bugs have a home here. And when I release my flower gifts many stop to admire. My flowers are my gifts to you! Well, of course they're necessary for me too, but they are my expression of joy: the "flowering of my personality." The worst thing about being here is the old growth parts which are dead weight that I must hold up. I like the feeling of rebirth through new growth. It's exhilarating, while the old is just so boring. It's as if the dead branches want to hold me back.

Having healthy branches cut away is not so nice. I ask, "Why?" I was having fun. But I understand that the way must be given to others. That's okay by me. We are many spirits. Each growth or flower embodies a spirit all its own but it transcends as that flower falls off. Then the spirit goes to other places, other trees.

The spirits of cut flowers often linger if they feel they can do some good. They might enjoy the experience of being among a new group of flowers and of pleasing people. Or they will go on their way and then the flowers usually die quickly. Yes, if there is a need, or a person who appreciates us, we might stick around.

I enjoy your beautiful fragrance!

To smell sweet is my job. I can take on a further life—many of us do—when my extracts are used. This pleases me. But I have been told that sometimes extracts are artificially imitated and that bothers me.

What about your connection to other trees?

Through the roots and soil there is communion. We can chat if we like but it's usually about the weather, or about something that went wrong. Otherwise, we are too happy just being ourselves and enjoying growth and rebirth. Love to you. We hope you are understanding of the local people here who really want to please but are often perplexed by you tourists and by their roles as you come to visit.

Banyan Tree

"My friend, without us you would not be here. We are Mother Nature's tenderness, her skin, her gladness; her gift of life in air, food and shelter."

This tremendous old tree, with branches spanning a huge radius, dominated a small hill near the city of Hamilton on the island of Bermuda. The banyan tree is fascinating for the way in which its roots grow down from upper branches, eventually reaching the earth and taking root. The result is a complex structure of intertwining limbs, spiraling, merging, and flying through the air as new connections are made to the ground.

You must be important being so large.

ut I did not start out so. I was only an offshoot, a little sprig when I claimed this site. It was perfect for me. Later they landscaped around me. What else could they do? Yes, all these branches are but one tree, just a large family. We need to keep expressing ourselves! There is much to do here, watching over this hill, spreading my arms for the pleasure of so many. I am not deciduous. The leaves come in waves with some growing in different cycles than others.

There are little palm trees growing up, around and through you.

They will be pruned soon enough as they seem to get in the way. You see, everybody wants to be with me! They "dress me up." There is only one way for me to grow—that's everywhere!…and big! I touch the sky! Pleasure, my friend, is my purpose!

I come from an ancient time. We were unruly then, only now many species have become plainer, simpler. I take root from above or the water would never travel up to my many mouths. It's a feeding thing, see? How else do you expect me to get fed to the ends of my branches from so far away?

Fondaton is my name you see. It means "many growths, much fun." I came here long ago to observe. It's not so very much fun to be among people who aren't happy. But here there was much joy from happy children hiding in me and playing many games. Then when the young ones grew up, new children came. And then *they* grew up. So I sat and pleasured myself all this time waiting for some of them to return, but now I am isolated on this hill.

What sorts of things don't you like?

There are waves of unpleasantness that arrive. Discontent and fear from people come in energy waves that get stuck to my branches. And smoke too. I take it all in but I remember a time when it was not this way. My job was easier then. I don't know if you can see them or not (the færies), but they are here and enjoy sitting with me, encouraging me.

Sometimes I wonder if it's all worth going on and I ask, "Why?" The færies joke with me, tease me and say, "You can't be serious—you must stay here and protect your position." They don't like to see any spot where there is no "coverage" of beautiful life and they especially like us old timers. We go way back!

At this point I was introduced to "Fanwright," who said he was one of the captains of Bermuda's plant life; the head færie in charge. I commenced speaking with this powerful creature, and asked him about his funny name and that of our mutual friend, Fondaton.

Fanwright: My friend, there are many funny names. Yours is funny to me. I have infinite patience for you. I've been here as long as the hills. I'm one of the captains of this island. Fondaton is tired. When you stay around a long time you have to eventually ask the question "why?" so he asks it now.

What of all these little palms growing around him?

They are "contenders" for this spot. They nudge him, help him feel that he is supporting them, but they are supporting him by giving of their life force and their encouragement.

But he is large and vital, look at all those leaves.

But he needs encouragement. You see, things have changed as he said. All the little children stopped coming around so these small palms and growths are his new companions.

Why is it so important to cover the earth with green?

Oh, my friend, without us you would not be here. We are mother nature's tenderness, her skin, the eruptions of her gladness, and her gift of life in air, in food, in shelter. This was the design, that all has been provided for you in her many species. Now you've not been satisfied. You are in competition with earth trying to do it all your own way! This is bad. Also unnecessary, because everything's already provided. Living off the trees and plants creates a cycle—a wonderful cycle of development. It used to be that way here until the white men came. They always knew better. You are one who likes to listen…but then you think you know better too.

Fanwright, how can I find a girlfriend?

God provides everything, my friend. When there is not enough water he brings the rain. He will nourish your soul but like I said, you think you know better. Now relax and let Him bring you her.

Just like my big friend here, continue to grow in the sun and love life itself. Then life shall bring her to you and she shall be one with life too, and you shall be happy. Don't push with feelings of emptiness because that only brings one who is empty herself. Choose to exude contentment over what you have already got, and for being provided for. Then know that in all ways shall the further supplying of your needs continue to take place as you desire. Thank you.

Giant Palm Tree

"There are many gardeners who really love us
and don't view us as design elements,
but honor the life in us."

*I left Fondaton, and I thought, Fanwright, and found myself
by the water in a place with the amusing name of Waterville Park. I
sat down on a bench, pen in hand, beside a huge palm tree.*

Fanwright: Going for the big ones? Think
they have more news to tell?

Me to palm: What's your story?

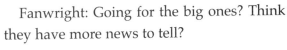 have been here a long time. The cold…this
weather is not so very cold, you know.
There's plenty of water here close to the surface so it gets to me easily and that's why we
all flourish. That's how it is on an island.

Do you have a name?

Fendbar.

Oh, you must know Fondaton.

We know of each other through Fanwright. He connects us
all through a gridwork of energetic patterns, a lighted structure

of connection that passes between us, like holding hands. We are all in agreement to give this place much nourishment.

Do you like living in these manicured gardens?

Yes, although we don't care to have people fooling with us, cutting us up, creating your idea, not ours, of what a garden should look like. But what we like is being cherished, paid attention to, given a sanctuary of specialness, being respected by people, rather than just being trampled upon or brushed aside.

Each one of these places, while artificial in design (kind of "man-ified," through man screwing up nature by doing it his way) is still special because it shows appreciation; a recognition that there is cooperation or synergy between us. In just this way we plants cooperate with one another. These gardens are a start. There are many gardeners who really love us and don't view us as design elements, but honor the life in us.

Impatiens
Rosebud Lavender

"Our spirits soar and play together.
There is a hum, a tone from our growing.
Can you hear it?"

In a commercial greenhouse in Bermuda I approached these young sprouts emerging from tiny starter pots which were lined up in nice, neat rows. I wasn't sure what these babies would have to say or even which one to address.

Who can I speak with here?

verybody. Hello. We know some things, other things we do not. We feel big in our little pots because the limits of them *are* our worlds.

What do you dream of?

We are, of course, anxious to be claimed, to grow well so someone will buy us and take us home, giving us extended life by repotting, etc.

You look bigger than the others.

I am happier. He was crushed; the seed wasn't so happy. Yes, it is most happy here in this home. Our spirits soar and play

together. There is a hum, a tone, from our growing. Can you hear it?

What about the formula of the soil?

The gardeners put something in it that helps us grow better but since it's an artificial stimulant, we look good although our patterns are changed from the normal. The natural way is preferable.

Where do you come from?

I come from the Father of us all. We don't know him but he's grand. It's enough to trust.

Is there a spirit over this nursery?

Oh yes, would you like to speak? It's a grand energy.

I met Sufis and asked him about the authoritarian quality I noticed in Bermudian society, extending from the government to the highly structured behavior of ordinary citizens.

Sufis: I am so large that my body is a blanket covering my little friends. Yes, this is a highly controlled place. That is the nature of this entire island, because if anyone should break the rules it seems to threaten the entire structure.

No one must ask, 'Why?' And it starts from above, passed on

from the original colonial government to the present one, so order and structure have been handed down. Do you see those neat little houses? Everything is just so. Well, they also like their "'plants,'" as you call them, to be contained and orderly. But at least they appreciate us so we agree to grow in their fashion and everything is okay with this arrangement. Yet, with any such structure, it has to fracture eventually if things are to keep growing—I mean growing in an evolutionary way.

Next, I went to interview one of the small potted palms which the nursery kept in neat rows outdoors behind a fence. Very quickly one of the proprietors kicked me out. Just to hear his reaction, I told him I was a plant psychic interviewing his palm trees. His response was, "Different!"

And as I walked away, down the road past a high hedge, I discovered that my new reputation had preceded me. "

"Hello," said the hedge, "you must be Fanwright's friend."

Peperomia Incana

"We all just know our names because the færies dub us as they come to greet us."

How does one select a single subject to interview out of the many interesting species in the greenhouse in Bermuda's Botanical Garden? This little leafy plant attracted me with its rounded leaves and velvety covering which felt so sensuous to the touch. Also, next to her was the only bench on which to sit.

e love the moisture on our leaves, and the feeling in this greenhouse is most serene and wonderful. Can you feel it?

Yes, and you are so soft!

Do you like it? We are happy you do. To really feel us, it's not necessary to touch, but you may touch us. We are spreading out in all directions to give thanks to the sun. To be us is a wonderful thing and it's even better to be around all the others: so many friends, all with their own energy.

Are there any plants here you don't like?

What do you mean? We each have a place. Perhaps in a

jungle there would be a vying for a better spot but here each has her place.

Why are some plants spiny, and some soft?

I guess I am representative of the soft side of life. This is my mission or my play at this time.

I asked the name of this unassuming creature and she replied, "Barbara." Feeling perplexed I thought this over, doubting what I'd heard, when a soft, insistent but somewhat defensive voice repeated:

Barbara! Once, someone came near to me and then called to her friend, "Oh, Barbara, look at this one," so I took that as my name. Do you like it? Tan-u-sed was my name before. We just know our names because the færies dub us as they come to greet us. Tan-u-sed means "one who has as much love to give as to receive."

If you must go now, thank you for your attention.

Indian Laurel

"I want to give to [Nature] what she has given to me and others: life and nourishment. What have I to give her?"

Commanding a grassy embankment just off a heavily trafficked circle in Bermuda, this huge tree with its wave-like ripples of endless roots, proved a willing and affable respondent. In this interview, the tree refers to my avant-garde American friends and me as being somewhat different than the local people.

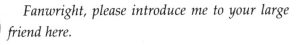

Fanwright, please introduce me to your large friend here.

anwright: Much obliged. He is one of my good tree friends. You can call him Tond-a-no.

Tond-a-no: I am very happy to meet you. I don't usually speak to people although so many come by and admire me. I wish that I could say, "Thank you," for all the compliments but I am just a tree. What can I say? So I stay around, listen, and bask in admiration.

Children love me. They say, "Oh mommy, I want to climb

that tree!" Most of the mothers around here are very proper and don't want their children to get hurt. I get climbed on seldom, except for the ants. I am their superhighway.

How do you like being here with all this traffic?

Well, you know, there is much more now than there used to be. It gets worse every year! But, do I mind it? Hmmm...I am used to it. I accept my place. I hold down this corner of the earth. It is my special home in which I have agreed to take root, and so I enjoy being here in this spot. Especially when you talk to me. This is the best!

Your long, swirling roots are fascinating.

I am trying to reach out and touch you, to spread my arms and legs as far as I may. There is that wall [in front of the sidewalk] that stops me, but I will go the other way.

I have already sent out many tendrils. I am like rippling water in the forms that I create because I send my energy out in pulses like a heartbeat. As every wave of energy extends out from my center it literally creates a ripple effect. I admire this about myself. It's time for me to relax now and bask in the love that I feel.

How old are you?

In earth years, I am seventy years old. In terms of my own winter, spring, summer, and fall, I am what you would call middle aged, but I am still most vital. I am thinking of a time towards my retirement, and I spoke about this with Fanwright, and the others. They like to have me around though. I am good "public relations" because I am so beautiful. Many people who don't admire trees say, "Oh, wow! Look at that one!"

What makes you unhappy?

Well, I become anxious when I am awaiting my friends the færies and spirits. They don't always come on time. They come in the morning after the sun has arisen. But sometimes I wait and they are late. I think they overslept. But I realize they have many like me to attend to. I worry every day even though they always show up. Other than that, I am happy.

Once I had a dream: I thought, if only I could be the biggest tree on the biggest hill [on earth] with no wall to stop me from growing. My many branches and leaves would spread out and out and out. I would not stop, for my legs and roots would grow deeper and deeper and deeper in the earth, further reaching the warmth of the Mother. I want to give her what she has given to me and others: life and nourishment. What have I to give her? So I decided that would be my way. These dreams come and go. And the next moment, a bird comes to join me and I listen to her song and my thoughts travel inward, away from such silly dreams, and I am once again reminded of myself and I say, "if this bird, and these ants like the house I provide then I must be a good house," and so I am happy again.

What do the færies do when they arrive?

It is like an awakening. A greeting for the new day. They dig their fingers into their little færie pots and take a handful of special powder. Then they wave their arms as they dance around and shower me with light and say, "Now you be good! What have you been doing? Did you miss us? We told you not to worry. We said we'd be right along. Oh, you!" They love to tease and that is why I love them.

Fanwright is right behind them. He stands and watches. Sometimes he will do a little dance and he seems to travel up my trunk and branches all at once, slithering like a snake. He says, "Is everything alright? Do you have a sore? What's the matter in this spot?" Then he gives me a kiss and I feel well.

What can we do for you right now?

I like your caresses. Tell the others to come and meet me and say hello. More friends! You are a little different, you and your friends. Many people are polite but not friendly around here. I mean, because they do not wish to be childlike. They will not allow themselves to engage in earthiness, silliness. They don't know what they are missing. They will find out in due time. These people will learn that it's us trees who add so much importance to their lives, not their autos. They would not even have homes if it were not for us. One by one they learn. The little girls, they know. "Oh mom! Look at that tree. It's so big!" I like them and send blessings on their little heads. I will do this for you too. I love you.

Do you mind when dogs pee on you?

Of course not. So what. I get a little wet. I like them because they like me. They are my friends too. Some of them are unhappy, really unhappy, because imagine if someone put a chain around your neck. Would you like that? They are like me . They wish to please and so they forget about it. They go about their business. Not too many dogs come over since I am far away from the sidewalk. I get some cats though. They will climb up. I like to feel the fur. It's a nice caress.

CHAPTER THREE

Random Facts of Ripeness

Aloe Plant

"A plant grows best with
somebody to appreciate it."

One day, looking for willing subjects, I went upstairs and interviewed my housemates' plants.

Are you being well taken care of here?

t's alright. You know, so much can make up for the deficiencies, the indignities we put up with. Just being here alive, and in the sun, makes us ignore some aches and pains. We don't want to be unhappy or complain. We don't complain. Who would listen? We'll need a transplanting soon. Hope it's soon. There's not enough pot, too much plant.

How does it feel being in a pot?

It is a matter of directing our energies. We don't live the same way as a plant in the earth soil. There are aspects pro and con. We get special treatment because we are one of only a few other plants here, but then we are confined, on display. We help green up the atmosphere, doing our cleansing work of course, but it's like being a lion in a cage. You can't get out and so you are just

to be looked at. Indeed, these two women who own us care. A plant grows best with somebody to appreciate it.

Now who am I speaking with?

We are some tantalizing færies who know oh so many things. We are speaking for this little plant. You should see us all around. We like your coming to us in this special way, but you are blind, really. Try looking with your senses; that is, your mind's eye.

I am an elf, a plant elf, out of water so to speak, here on the third floor, away from the earth. I'll return to my home in the tree trunk soon. I came for you. But we're not here because you believe us to be. We are here despite you and before you. I am a million years old, you know.

Do you die then return again?

No, I'm not physical like you so there's nothing to grow old or decay. I have but one little job to fulfill and that's all I need. My name is Borison. No, not "poison" (laughs)! I am the little elf of this room. I come to make the plants happy. They are already happy without me though. As I care for them my spirit soars high from love of my job. Do you want to move on? I won't interrupt. Goodbye.

A Dying Plant

"It is pleasurable to be slowly ending,
feeling the life pulse slowly ebb."

I came upon this plant at my dentist's office. No one there was able to identify its species. Unfortunately, it was nearly check-out time for this withered and forlorn creature, an anomaly in the office where a multitude of other potted plants appeared to flourish.

Are you not well?

t is my time to go. I don't want to disappoint so I try to hang on. There is a pleasant sensation for me in "crossing over" so you should-n't interrupt me in this process. There is root rot, old soil, no interest. I must move along.

Once, I was once the centerpiece in this office, but I have been overshadowed. I was the initiator in this space. Now I pass the torch to the "young folk."

It is, as I said, pleasurable to be slowly ending, feeling the life pulse slowly ebb, and making my transition. I could be revived by taking a new cutting and repotting with fresh soil in a new

pot. Then another being would come in for a new life. My plant is waning. Thank you for explaining this to [the dentist] for me. I do not wish to disappoint.

Thank you for this time. I do wish that a cutting be taken to extend this entity's life though I, its soul, go on. Do not mourn this passing.

Purple Flowering Shrub

*"I will always be the little purple light, I guess.
Then sometime I'll be back in another way."*

*I was attracted to a patch of small shrubs with vivid purple
flowers that had been planted near a Farmer's Market. There were
many potential interviewees to choose from but (as usual) I chose a
comfortable spot where I could sit and chat.*

hat is it? I'm okay, but I don't feel so well. It's
cold. I can't happen [grow] this way. All of us
feel the same, but I get even less light in this
corner. Thank you for saying I'm interesting.
This color is my own. It's how I express. Yes
sir, that's me, very pretty when my buds are young and bright.
Oh that's nice [*I began stroking its leaves*]. It's interesting to be
held. I like it.

I don't know if they'll just uproot me. They do that. A new
season and they just pull you up, put in new friends. I think
they should try to keep you, add water. But I'm old. It's my
time; this is coming to an end.

Where will you go?

I will always be the little purple light, I guess. Then sometime I'll be back in another way.

I want to grow stronger, longer, be around more sun, more appreciation. It's cold here but not just the weather. We feel cold, unloved. It seems we are just a background pattern. We know there is more to life than this. I don't want anything except to be. . .to be happy. You are the first to care, to ask. Thank you. Yes, in another spot, back in the greenhouse we were all young, strong, warm. There was a person there, a young girl, just a daughter, who appreciated us. Not for money, you see. And we all had fine expectations then.

There's another thing: we could give you energy for that hand. [*I had recently fallen while roller skating, hurting my hand.*] It's like us, some limbs go finished. Yes, smell us and be strong! That is our gift. It attracts the bugs who help. But they don't come now. Too cold, we told you.

Your coming has added something to this life. I guess that's why you came to me. I called the loudest.

Saguaro Cactus

> "Humans must not go where they are not invited or welcomed. And if they enter a place as guests, they must behave with respect."

"Why are the Saguaro Cactuses Dying?" asked the headline on an Arizona newspaper. I didn't pick it up to find out. But I'd asked myself the same question as I drove through Phoenix toward Flagstaff and saw the unhappy state of virtually every one of these large and proud desert creatures. Their stalks were grey and pockmarked, and some of their "arms" sagged from their own weight. I became motivated to learn the answer to the newspaper headline from the Saguaros themselves. By the side of the road I located a healthier-looking Saguaro and interviewed it.

es, we can speak. I'll talk if you like. I'm a happy cactus plant.

Why are you happy? I see a few grey spots there on your shady side.

I am happy here in the sun. Oh, these spots, these places don't affect me much. They are just a part of nature.

What's the purpose of a cactus?

We serve many purposes. We express life for ourselves, we express abundance and also are sources of energy and water in that we draw up those small reserves to make them available to others. But we also need sharp spines for protection or we wouldn't survive. Creatures would peck at us unmercifully.

What about all the unhealthy-looking cactuses?

We hear you asking the question. Shall we answer what you already know? There is a disease of Cactuses similar to what has been termed "AIDS." It's becoming difficult to resist environmental pollution and we, who stand as symbols of the vitality of the desert; who represent life despite the absence of water, have had about all we can take of cars and pollution and radiation.

We are taking a stand to show that things are dying everywhere. It is our agreement, you see. It is the cactuses' agreement to tell the world what we can from our position here. Trees are making their own statement and this is our message to you to let you know things are not as they should be.

There will be many of us cactuses who will succumb, die off, fall over. But the species is hearty and cannot be made extinct at this time. We, who so represent the desert, may return when mankind has wisened up and learned to respect the earth's natural gifts.

So, even in such a barren place as a desert there is yet life to offer hope. We offer hope to those who know us and a warning for those who don't. We say, "Look out!" or discover what you've taken for granted will soon be gone. There are things you don't know about going on in the earth, like nuclear waste. This is becoming worse and so we will say goodbye in an apocalyptic move to make people listen.

Notice that the other desert plant life continues to flourish because it is our decision to take this stance, not theirs, for we are kings of this domain.

What would you most like to change?

Humans must not go where they are not invited or welcomed. If they enter a place as guests, they must behave with respect, not mess up the guest quarters. *You* wouldn't do that. But there are so many who view themselves as the true leaders of the planet because their money makes them think they have ultimate control of the world. They think they are smarter because of it, and can do as they please. *Please* don't think that you can go anywhere and do anything to destroy our desert when you haven't cleaned up your other places. Don't dump on us! What you can do is honor us and not interfere. We know we are just a small part of the plan, and we are glad indeed to do our part. Then time will see what happens, but we shall not be lost for we will return in full flower when the time is right.

As for you, you are telling our story to the world? This is good. You may also feel like shutting down at times in protest, or feel like hiding, but we suggest you are one whose job it is to tell. And for this you shall be protected. We bless your efforts and are glad you came to us. Thank you.

CHAPTER FOUR

California Blooming

Privet Tree

"I like to blossom myself in my leaves of love."

Somebody must have thought that the once stately Privet trees lining the residential end of Beverly Hills' Rodeo Drive were too exuberant for their own good. When I passed through the area, I was horrified to see that all the upper branches of these trees had been amputated. They were all leafless and stumpy, yet apparently still alive. How did the Privet trees feel about this situation? I asked.

h, I am very happy, sir!

Even though you've been all chopped off?

Yes, we all have. It doesn't matter. They think it is helpful to cut us back. As you can see, we may still grow, and find a route to come up by [to blossom].

We like to spread our roots deeply to reach as far as possible. It gives us a strong foundation, a good grip, and it allows us to balance the top growth.

What happens when they cut your branches short?

Oh, it hurts; we are full of indignation at first, the wind fresh

against the cut ends feels strong. It burns, then the healing begins and we start to push in other directions. As you can see, we may grow very strong and tall. Too tall they say.

I am one who doesn't mind. I have a rich spot here by the park. The playing children…it is so very nice here, although it's rather busy with all the traffic and activity. It's cluttered with noise, but I feel good every day when the sun beats down. I like the shade too. I like to blossom myself in my leaves of love. I feel clothed then. I feel good. I want to be clothed again as more leaves come. Don't you also like to do the best you can?

Have you a far different personality than your other tree friends?

I am myself, yes. This is true. How could it not be so? I think my own thoughts, but I also share them. You might say I'm influenced by the others. We all decide together. Everybody here [all species of plants and trees] are one—we all agree. Things have been nice here for us.

Please tell me about the recent earthquake here.

You mean the ground moving? If I say it feels rather good will you believe me? Before it happened the færies came by to tell us. Oh yes, they knew about it. So we braced ourselves. We were ready. I think everybody knew, except the people. The færies said it was necessary to release pent up energy. So when it came I rolled along. Short. It's so very brief. Are you worried about another one? You'll be okay.

Anything else you'd like to say?

I'm not sure I can say anything much. Here it is: love yourself as you are. If you lose a limb, then still love what's left, as I do. We all do. There is nothing else for it but acceptance. Some feel regret or get angry when things don't go the way they want them to. I just imagine myself fully clothed in beauty and then I am.

Eucalyptus Tree

"We feel that so many humans are afraid
of becoming out of step. . .and fearful
of taking a wrong turn."

Amidst frisbee players and happily romping dogs, I sat in San Francisco's panhandle portion of Golden Gate Park and interviewed this huge old tree.

You've been here a long time. Please tell me about yourself?

What do you want to know? Yes, I feel you, little one. I feel your little hand against me as I have felt so many hands coming to touch; so many paws upon me. How long have I been here? Too long! I have many joys and only a few sorrows. I look about and think of what was, and the changes that have taken place in the fabric of your society. I do not know the details. But I see the people and I feel the mood in the sky, in the air. I see the air becoming foul. I see the people becoming foul like the air. Well, we all breathe in the same air do we not? So if it is foul, you will be foul. But I am not mad or foul. No, this is something I observe and look at in wonder. And

2

b

a

I do wonder, sometimes, why I am here? But this place that I have been planted is a sacred plot. And I am most proud that I am so big, and so old, and that I've been here so long. I am a living reminder of past times. Bit I have locked away such memories and do not dwell upon them for there is so much more happening every day.

Do you not want to hear this? Is there something else? What have I seen? I have seen the changes, the clothes, the cars, the noise, Oh! the noise! This has changed so much, you should only have heard what it was like in the past from the clanking of carts in the streets to today's cars rushing... Never this much noise. But it is not these physical changes that I am trying to describe. I am trying to tell about the mood; the feelings in the air that I experience. There is something unsettled... as though people are in constant transition, waiting for the next earthquake, waiting for the next plague, feeling as if they're not in control; not feeling the masters of their own destinies, as though others control them.

There is such an attitude of letting it be, of letting it all happen to them and simply riding with the wave. This is what we see. Yes, there was a time when the men walked by and they were in charge of their lives. Oh, you might ask, what were they really in charge of? This is true, for you all walk around with your heavy burdens, your heavy cares. But in the past, the people put one foot in front of another, stepping forward with assuredness. They were making a path with their feet as they forged ahead, whereas now we see so many who are merely following in the footsteps of those earlier ones.

We feel that so many are afraid of becoming out of step; of stepping out into a place that they are forbidden. People today are fearful of making a wrong turn or a wrong move. I do not have such fears. I can only do one thing which is to stand here, grow strong and simply observe. Oh yes, I watch. I watch the people who come to play and to walk and to wonder and to juggle, and to throw the balls and the frisbees; and I watch the dogs who run around.

You should be like the dogs: they care not. They carry not with them the burdens of heavy concerns, They follow, as I do, the master's voice. Only they have a different master. Yes, their master is a human to whom they attach themselves. My masters are the Creator, the earth, the moon, the sun. If I could tell you about some of the interactions I enjoy with these you would be surprised, for you only know the tip of the iceberg, my friend. You think you were the first to engage my intellect?

I understand what you're saying. Tell me, are you an old soul?

Old soul indeed. Older beyond this life that you rest upon. Before I was here, I was still me. I rested many, many, many æons. I felt myself pulled into awareness from the spark of the molten beingness. And then *I was!* And when my soul, my essential being, became focused into but a radiant seedling— just a fraction of the whole—I was then lovingly placed here.

Oh, I had a birth just as you do, that is to say, I had a birth into form just as you experience. I bring my spark into it just as you enter the organic matter, the lifeless form. Thus was I pollinated as the life force into the seedling, which enabled this tree to form that which I am. You want to know why I continue to grow? You want to know about the other spirits in my existence, about my conscious relationships with other sentient beings? I will tell you for there are so many. The earth and the sun are just two of them.

Do you not think there is intelligence in this sun; in this pulsating energy which comes down upon me to enjoy as others do? Yes, we would call these quantum fragments, segments of information, if you will: encodements to unlock certain key structures of information upon the reaching of my being. Yes, we are thinking of your CDs and their little encodings. The persons who invented that process were inspired, for this is a digital or a hieroglyphic representative encoding of information. This is not information. These are symbols of information. The sun's rays—the pulses that beat upon you and me—unlock their information in just such minute fragments and yet they are not symbolic of information. They *are* information. Just try to unlock such codes. You will be a million years in doing so! Yet there are those, the physicians, the angels, and the outer spacelings who come, who look upon you. They work with such energies and know such codes.

We know you can comprehend such activities, for you have witnessed the birth of so much technology and the exponential increase in growth of such systems of relating information. There is so much more yet to come.

I am most happy to have met you and to have you come and talk to me in a way that so few seem to be able or interested to do. I am a big, big tree and I am happy and proud to be here in this place for I have seen much joy. I hope that we'll meet again.

Philodendron Speciosa

"If you have plants in your house consider them friends because that's what they are."

Huge leaves from this amazing plant, some four to five feet in length, hang down above the heads of visitors to the San Francisco Conservatory located in Golden Gate Park. An amazingly complex web of spiralling tendrils surrounds the main trunk. Roots start from above and grow toward the ground where they eventually take hold in the soil. The sign says that this "Imperial" specimen came from Brazil and was planted in 1883.

 e will speak with you. We think you're amazing too. Oh, it's no trouble for us to grow this way. We just keep sending off shoots. If you see us in the jungle where everything is big we wouldn't seem so out of place.

So we came here and everyone says, "Ah!" Now we are a spectacle. If you must know, we keep growing, keep coming forth to show off because we get encouragement. You have no idea how nice it feels here, and with all the people coming to exclaim! We don't care about running out of space to grow. It hasn't happened yet. Our friend comes [grows] too. We plants are all friends. I do like when people touch me gently. You touch to feel, to connect with my life energy, to feel it within you. Others just want to pull.

I see you've been cut off here and there.

Oh, that won't stop me! I keep right on. Don't you see, I'm everywhere! This [Conservatory] is very old. I was here first! I know these walls. They keep trying to fix the place up but don't know what to do about us. They think we'll suffer. How could we?! It's too grand in here. I get such energy from all the appreciation. That's what I thrive on!

See, here are more well-wishers. Really, they should just come out and be in the jungle. Then they'd see so much more. But everyone can't travel that far.

What don't you like?

I sometimes see angry people, those who don't treat their kids with respect, and this I am sad for. I treat every part of myself with love and tenderness. I am many and I am one, like your hair. My individual parts grow all together.

What would you like to tell everyone about yourself?

About myself there is nothing much to say, but I'd like to tell all to think of us as your friends, and not separate from yourselves; not so different as you for we respond to you. Touch us with gentleness. It's nicer that way.

If you have plants in your house consider them friends because that's what they are.

Why do your stems wrap around yourself?

It protects and it makes me happy. That is all I know: to hug myself. I don't make the rules. I just follow and grow. It's fun to be here and be seen.

Cannabis

"Marijuana is such a funny word,
a little girl's name. A cute name for such
'vicious' creatures as we."

Quiz. Name a plant which: grows up to sixteen feet in one season; produces the finest quality linen and paper; has been used for centuries as medicine, is among the most nutritious foods available; produces high-quality fuel oil...and is illegal. If you guessed cannabis, or marijuana, you are a well-informed and progressive individual (or simply read the title above). I located some friends who were growing some marijuana and who allowed me to interview it.

ur job is to come forth beautifully and strongly. We are, as many have suggested, the salvation of the planet. But we are not alone since all life holds different promises and different purposes. When you look at all of nature's creatures together, we form a perfect whole. We all work together in harmony so we do not see ourselves as special.

We are to be part of the emergence of the new social order. One which is to be expanded not by governments but by ordinary people searching for their own truth. As this becomes wider spread, you will find that many things you do not yet have an inkling of—other medicinal plants, other new healing technologies—will be breaking through, coming back, becoming respected again to ever increase the healing that is going on.

Why are you so wise and broadminded?

We are speaking to you not merely from the little plant itself but from the broad overview of the spirits who guide and watch over the various plants of this species throughout the world. As cannabis devas, it is our job not only to take care of this plant, but we have been given a certain higher authority than other plant devas because of the value that these plants offer and because of the political turmoil that has erupted.

What are the true reasons behind the suppression of marijuana?

Marijuana is such a funny word: a little girl's name. A cute name for such "vicious" creatures as we. Is this not a paradox? We do not think we are at fault in such matters. The real issue is people's abilities to express themselves freely. And we have become a symbol of freedom, as indeed many will wear the leaf symbol of the marijuana plant to indicate they are of a different mindset than others. They are in a sense branding themselves, or showing themselves to be outlaws.

One of our many characteristics is to be mind-expanding. Many substances found in nature have a similar effect of providing the user with a greater overview, one which does not allow thought to be limited or confined. This is seen as threatening to the establishment. This is the real reason for our suppression, not because we are a paper substitute.

Under our influence there can be a lack of respect for authority. Those who partake of our oils, our energy, often do not wish to take themselves too seriously. Our purpose is also to enhance the clarity of one's focus as opposed to deadening or confusing it like cocaine which creates a euphoric state, but not a positive frame of mind.

What about the medicinal uses of the cannabis plant?

All things have their purposes and unique functions. Ours are manifold. We have been used widely in medicine for we have the ability to create a clearing within the body. Whether to clear blockages in the eyes, or in nasal and throat passages; to expand in the lungs, or the consciousness; this is our mission and function.

We are a demonstration of the simplicity that abounds. We

show that you need not resort to complex machinations to accomplish your goals. All of these things we are here to teach.

There will be an increasing demand for this product for reasons other than "getting high" and this will eventually turn the tide in one State after another until there is a general acceptance. This will be one of the areas in which the government will simply throw up its hands and say, "Oh, let them at least have *this*." From then on we can proliferate.

May we now speak to the plant itself?

[*The plant speaks:*] I am most happy to be a part of this interview and the focus of this talk. It is unusual for me to have such an honor bestowed upon me. The visiting emissaries who have made themselves known to you are important devas. They are instrumental in pursuing the goals that many humans are also working towards. It has made me happy to be the entry point for these ones of whom I have known and have been aware, but with whom I've not had the privilege to be so close.

I feel proud and strong to serve you and grow strong for you and grow to your expectations. I must confess I also feel important in my position in the sun, near the door of this house. I feel as though I am, in a sense, taking care of you.

I feel within me a connection to the many, many plants of my species around the world. We have a group mission. There is a celebration when more of us are allowed to come forth, even though it may be in a secretive manner.

What message do you want to tell the world?

It will be very difficult to eradicate us. For at the same time there is a resurgence of interest, even many of the police who would confiscate our buds would take them into their own homes to enjoy just as you would.

We find that the future of the new world is not a continuing growth of large corporations but a growth of small communities which will then break up into other small communities. Each will be like tribes of Native Americans. Each will have its farmers, its newspaper, it's cobbler. Each individual will be answerable to his or her community so there will not be the corruption one finds when the larger producers and corporations lose sight of the fact that they are just as human as those they are producing for. This is what we see happening in the future and hemp will be a part of this as we are so prolific. We are a gift to all of you in these times.

MIRACLE

GROWN
IN U.S.A.

Krishnamurti's Orange

"How divorced you are from the earth
that it brings a thrill when you see us in
our natural state of growing!"

*The entrancing scent of orange blossoms filled the air as I drove
past the luscious orange orchards of Ojai, California. When I arrived
at the Krishnamurti Library where that great teacher had lived, I could
hardly resist pilfering an orange (alright, two!) from a tree on the
library grounds. This is what one of those oranges had to say:*

ou have taken me from the bliss of the sphere
to a place I have not known. But I feel welcomed by you and I look forward to serving
you through my nourishment. I am anxious
to move along my path for I understand my
future in the afterwards; in the great vastness of eternity.

What can you tell me about Ojai and the people who live there?

The people in this town love their way of life. They've all
come, attracted by the unspoiled nature and peace. But they
soon begin to take over and coincidentally threaten our existence. Humans don't mean to upset nature (so we cannot blame

them). As they come near they tend to take over. Then it's as if we become a quaint decoration. Some people would rather see this "real estate," now covered in fruit orchards, utilized in other ways. So we oranges are riding along on the currents of such thoughts. It is distressing for we have known this life for so long. It seems horrible to just uproot the living beings here.

Don't you feel secure within the Krishnamurti library?

This library was blessed by the energy of the man and his ideals. Before he left we all were imbued with the lasting light of his radiance. I am happy that you were so drawn to us that you wanted a "free sample." And that we appealed to you, friend. How divorced you are from the earth that it brings a thrill when you see us in our natural state of growing! You experienced the bliss and serenity of our fields as you drove through. Just imagine if you had stayed with us for awhile.

[*An Orange Flower Færie speaks:*] I am the sweet one whom you smelled as you passed my way. My blanket of love transfixes all who attend these places that I oversee. I do not speak but tickle my friends and hover over them like the hot summer winds. We appreciate this homage you pay us, dear sir. We wish others like yourself would do us this honor.

CHAPTER FIVE
To The Redwood Forests

Redwood Tree

"From time to time be a tree. Think of us and exult in the stillness as you find yourself emulating our proud grandeur."

At Cascade Falls in Mill Valley, California, my mother accompanied me to interview this Redwood. We started by addressing any nearby tree devas.

Hello! Are there any tree spirits around here?

ello, glad to have you upon our little throne addressing us today. The answer is: yes! And we are many! We have a very important mission for plant life on Earth and for these trees in particular. We think you realize how important plant life is to humans, and that we are more than just beautiful, stately old growths. But other humans may not realize it as they chop it away, pave it over, and dig it up. Others create pleasant little garden spaces which please them; with which they control nature and make it in their own vision, instead of letting it run rampant the way we like it.

Do you think the placement of plants in the wild is all arbitrary? No, there is a more complex structure than you can imagine as to the positioning, and as to individual growths. We keep track of all this; it is all plotted. We place each in just the proper spot. And we bless each individual plant and growth.

Why do some plants flourish and others do not?

Well, how do you know that they do not flourish at some point, or that their purpose was not to establish a stand, or even to contribute a root base or opening for future growth, or to create organic matter to fertilize for the future? It's not as haphazard as you might imagine.

What do want from us humans?

We have been anxiously waiting for those like yourselves to come to us in reverence and in awe of our beauty. Many, of course, do come to these forests for just this purpose, but there often is not the full recognition of what it is that creates the beautiful feeling one gets in our presence. There is merely the reflection that it feels good to be here. There is rarely the feeling of communion or partnership between humans and us plants and plant spirits.

We do not require praise. We do not require much of anything from you, but that does not mean we are not happy when we receive it. When we see those coming to "hug a tree" or chain themselves to our trunks (in our defense), it gives us great joy and pleasure. Through the centuries we've merely done our jobs and fulfilled our duty to create growth and abundance. If you want to see abundance, this is it! We are evidence of the abundance of the earth and what we share is also yours to own and share.

We have seen times in which humans did respect and revere us for our work. You are now in a cycle which is returning to such appreciation. This will create a greater interaction between us. The Creator placed us all in this synergistic relationship, for you would not exist without us (hard though it may be for your human egos to comprehend).

Now, we'd like to turn you over to one of our friends here, and it shall be the one behind you who can speak to you now. We will come back if you like, or may meet you in another part of this world or this area. Bless you both for your communal spirits and your reverence and love for our work. We also appreciate your work and wish to tell the mother that she helps growth as we do. She nurtures growth; creates life and builds strong and tall creatures and in this we truly share a communion. We share this special bond with all the women of the earth.

So now we will turn you over to our friend here.

[*Redwood tree:*] Yes? Yes, I'm listening. What would you have me tell you, that I enjoy myself? That I'm rather content and happy upon this little bluff? I have many friends who come to visit and those who come to stay like the animals and the bugs who make their home in and around me. If you ask what I'm doing here, I might have to ask you the same. We're all just having fun and doing our jobs. What is my job? If I told you it is just to grow strong and to honor the earth that feeds me and sends me shooting up, up, would you say that it is not enough? And yet, what would you say of yourself and your goals and aspirations? What is their basis? Where are you coming from; what is it that you seek?

If we look past the specifics of your human goals and desires, we see many little lights, many faint hopes and dreams which appear to us as colors, little patches of color floating around you. We would say these are nothing more than human fantasies or the effects of exercising your free will; your will to want; your playing with your prerogatives, to ask for and then to venture forth into new and better intrigues and adventures. We are more content with our given path for, you see, we are not as unbounded as you. We accept [what would seem to you] the rather limited options of our lives. Yet, do we experience any less joy or fulfillment? No indeed!

If you strip away all of those needs that you feel so attracted to, the cars, the things, the love you feel devoid of, you might recognize that your basic needs are not so dissimilar from mine. You also want to grow, be happy and be appreciated. I'm appreciated every day in the sun that shines upon me and the water that rises up through my trunk, being drawn all the way up—it's an evaporative process—from the heat at the top causing it to rise. It is quite well designed.

As I waited, as a little sprig, a small offshoot, to reach the skies, to enjoy my own place among the others; I strove to become big and strong and this was my goal. Did I have doubts that I would ever make it? Well, I'll tell you, there were a few fires that came awfully close. I felt the smoke, but I survived and…it's true as they say that these fires can be necessary. They do destroy much, but they actually create a renewal. They open up for rebirth. They deposit rich nitrogen for new growth. It is much like your own death and rebirth. There's little difference.

Do not be afraid to touch me. You can't hurt me. Yes, I feel that. You may not think that I am so sensitive, but more than your touch, I feel the warmth coming from your being.

And now, what would the lady like to ask?

I would like to be able to practice non-doing the way you do. Is it possible within the framework of our human lives, to be non-doing, accepting, and not struggling all the time?

Ah well, we haven't as many options as you do. Our path is more defined. Don't think that I don't have stress at times. I worry about this or that as I see people passing by hurriedly and I wonder what it is that they're doing and what's going on in their lives. I will sometimes fret or complain: it's not going fast enough, it's too cold. Where are all the people? Why is no one coming by? Where are the animals? There are fewer now, yes. These are some of the things I wonder about. You have little legs to walk about on and see many things that I shall never see. You go many places and travel very far. And now you say you wish to be a tree?! (This is a tree joke.)

You seem so grand and majestic, and perfectly formed, like you know what to do. And we're still struggling. Does that make you a higher form of life? Not in the pun sense, of course!

You would make me blush. You make me draw back in joy from your words. I am not used to such kindness and I appreciate what you have said. Um, I do not know "higher." I know different. You have your job to do. I have my job to do. There are different jobs which are all designed by the Creator and so I hope you will do your job as well as I do mine.

You have asked, how to be a tree? How to do what a tree does? What you mean is how to be content. How to bring to yourself such a grand and satisfied, self-contained stillness as we seem to possess. We are content partly because of our nature which is more constrained than yours. For the gift of the intellect, the expressive intellect which you possess (which is different from ours) burdens you some in that you are forced always to express in ways that we may never do (until lovely ones as yourselves come around to talk to us).

For you to feel content you must simply not feel as though you need more than you have; or that you must be doing, doing, doing. For what does it gain you? Surely you will attend to your body, your needs. You will feed yourself in the manner that you must, cumbersome though it may seem to us who receive our nourishment almost automatically.

From time to time be a tree. Think of us and exult in the stillness as you find yourself emulating our proud grandeur. Think of us in our glory, if you will, in the joy of just being. For you wallow too much in self pity, in sorrow and agony. You agonize over the tiniest things, dear, worrying far too much. If you only knew that your plan too is outlined…and there is another thing. I do not worry about my fellow trees. They are served as am I by the loving, tender forces of nature, the spirits who dwell in these regions; who guarantee our lives. And so have you, larger, even more glorious [spirit guides], such as those about you now: glowing golden figures, clinging to my side as we speak.

So be not any different than a tree. Revel in your beingness and think of us, if it pleases you, and by so doing you may find yourself joining in our world of contentment.

What is your name?

You may call me whatever you like. That is enough. As for my friend [*the spirit deva who opened the interview*], call him Coralon.

Bushwark, the Disgruntled Redwood

"It doesn't mean much to have
you people come and say, 'Oh, how big!'"

I think that I shall never see a tree as disgruntled as this one. One of only a few giant redwoods along the walking path in Northern California's Muir Woods not situated behind a fence, this tree had apparently suffered the indignity of thousands of groping tourists' caresses. My adult daughter accompanied me to Muir Woods to ask questions for the following interviews.

Do you like it here?

o I like it here? What do you mean? I've been here so long, I forgot when I came. I just keep being here. That's all there is to it. Where do you want me to go?

Tree, are you unhappy? You sound annoyed.

No. I do not know this word "annoyed." But you people you come...so many people! And then you just go away and you don't come again. What do you want of me? It's like church.

You go there and say, "Oh how wonderful." But then, what do you do? Then you light matches, and you cut down trees! You sit on us in your chairs, you build with our wood! You really don't care. What proof have I that you care?

Oh, it's something to be a tourist attraction and it's something to be protected here, but I do not feel so glad that I am simply one of the safe ones, for I think of so many others who are not safe. Is this the story that you wanted? Did you want me to be all peace and light? I am this too. You got me on a bad day.

How does a good day differ from a bad day for a tree?

There are certain times when one is more in the flow than others. I have become distressed and saddened by situations because the færies come and they tell me, "You should see what happened! They're chopping away more and more."

But tree, don't you think there's also a lighter side, that more people are becoming enlightened and appreciating and valuing nature?

Yes, I guess you're right. There's that too. There are people like yourselves who appreciate trees, but you also have a certain arrogance. You think you can just walk up and say hello, and I'm expected to answer you. What do you think I'm here for? Your pleasure? For whatever you wish? No, don't go away.

I'm just venting.

Do you pay attention to human history? Is that important to you?

You mean the story of *your* lives? What about the story of my life? You wish me to know just about what happened to you? About your wars and your crimes and your times? You ask me as though I should know, as though I should care about these things?

(This is the angriest tree I ever talked to)

There you go, I am trying to tell you...how about asking about my life? What I feel?

Okay, how do you feel? What's your earliest memory?

I do remember some of those people you call Indians coming by. Now these people walked softly. They did not try to mess around with what is. They were almost apologetic as they traipsed through the forest hunting, gathering. They were much happier than you. They did not have such complicated auras. They did not have the flux, the muddiness. Much purer souls, like animals but with more intelligence, for they respected and understood the cooperation with all of nature. I appreciated that. And they mostly seemed to appreciate me. But you know it doesn't mean much to have you people come and say, "Oh how big!" This is not what I'm interested in.

Do you like animals? Like squirrels and stuff?

Oh yes, but you should know there are far, far fewer animals than there used to be. You have scared them away. This is what I'm talking about. That you come here to make everything your way; the way you like it. You build your fences, you "manage" our growth. This is annoying. And then you scare the animals away. Some still come, the birds and the bugs, but *you* like it clean. You like it without them about.

You have upset the natural balance of nature, and the weather and everything. And then even when you try to make it nice, when you try to right the wrongs you still try to make it your way. And this is what I'm bitter about. This is what I'm talking about. What else do you want to ask?

Can you feel me touching you?

Oh yes. I like you. I think you are nice. So is your father. Don't think I'm not happy about your coming to ask me such questions, but you see, it's been a long time since I got a chance to speak to you and tell you how I feel. I'm glad that you are willing to listen. So many others are not. So I'm happy to have you in my forest. Wait, you asked a question... I feel you but not in the way you think. I feel light and warmth. I feel the presence of your body near me. It's not so much that I feel a tip tap upon my skin. You understand? But what I do feel is the warmth coming through you which you are sending to me. I am grateful for the appreciation and respect that you are giving me.

Do you feel close to the trees around you? Do you talk?

You want to know what we speak about? It is a kind of happy reassurance to one another. Just to say, "yes, I am here another day, I love you and I feel you and you are healthy and yes, so am I." All this takes place not in words as you'd think for we do not converse in words but communicate in energetic patterns which emanate from us as we grow. And with each pulse, it sends out an energy wave of happiness. What you would call "growing larger" we would call expression of our need to create and fulfill ourselves. So with each such pulse of joy that is sent out, we reassure each other to continue to grow.

At this point, the battery in my tape recorder went dead without my realizing it. When we asked the tree its name it said, "Bushwark." Later it proudly boasted, "All the trees in the forest know Bushwark!"

No. 113

The Great Council of the Redwoods

"Many who are out of touch with their earth connection, feel threatened by nature."

As my daughter and I continued along the path in Muir Woods, a group of redwoods circling a small clearing seemed to beckon to me. This is what they had to say.

e think you are not surprised by what you have heard, nor surprised that, like you, trees have many different points of view.

We would like to scream to the people of this earth about preserving these species, but we also understand that you have your own agenda. We would like to tell you that despite whatever happens, we will outlive you. As much as some humans may be trying to, you cannot destroy us.

Many who are out of touch with their earth connection, feel threatened by nature. To them, we are too omnipresent, too large and too great in our scope. They would destroy us almost in an attempt to destroy the God who created us. And as they wield their saws and axes in their angry revenge, and in their near-sighted focus, thinking only of themselves and their human needs, they may destroy large sections, but we come back. And when they destroy that again we come back and when they defoliate and pollute the earth, yet do we come back!

This is why we feel sad that you humans have not been able to appreciate us on terms that we prefer, although you are but a small time blip in our existence. We have seen so much more, and have been here so much longer, and this period in which you effect your presence upon us is but a short space of time.

Some of us want to encourage you not to worry since your impact upon us is not very great. Moreover, we hold no grudges. We will continue to support you and to support all life, for this is our mission over which we have almost no choice. We do so in joy and love and this maintains us, so that we are not dependent upon you. We are solid and whole even as we go about our business and allow you to maintain yours. It would be easy to point the finger—our *many* fingers—and say you have done this, that and the other. You have burned us and turned away from us... but that would be of no use and would be but a minor criticism as we see it. For, in truth, you do not threaten us.

Are you saying that the people who are environmentalists should not waste their time?

Not at all, for they spawn a community of friends of the earth. We shall watch and see which community develops, whether it is the one in favor of the earth or the one seemingly against earth, who are fighting against their own creation, so to speak, wishing to overturn and overrule the forces of nature; to mold it to their own selfish design.

The park ranger wanted us to ask if you trees are doing alright?

Oh, you think that your minor interruptions affect us? You do not realize that we've been here under a variety of conditions for thousands of years and shall continue to maintain ourselves. We would hope that you would look upon our longevity as proof that we shall continue to exist. For you see, there is very little that can alter our life support system which is the earth itself. We will continue to grow under promising circumstances or as well under adverse conditions. Either way, we will continue our mission, so it matters not if humans try to plan our growth. We maintain ourselves just as we are and need no help from you for we have done without it for so many years.

We might say that we are amused that you set aside certain portions of land as special places for us, for every place is special to us. We would hope that more will come to understand this. So the answer to your question is that we are well.

I'd like to know whom we've been speaking to?

You have just heard from the communal legion of the redwood forests centered a bit north of here. We have heard of your mission to inform the earth of our intelligence, of the intelligence of all living species, and we are anxious to cooperate with you...so that you may print upon our pages these words of hope and of love. (We are merely pointing out this irony that you chop us down for paper so you may disseminate our words of wisdom and our concerns to others.) The Great Council of the Redwoods is our name. We appreciate your support.

Roedro the Redwood

"Our legs keep us rooted in the earth where all answers are automatically given."

Along a smaller path in Muir Woods, my daughter and I visited another giant Redwood who called himself Roedro.

How do you like being in this park?

h I like it very much. I think many happy people come here. It makes them happier to be here and I like to contribute to that. You've already spoken to the Great Council. Why would you want to speak to me?

It is difficult to say when I first came here, for I have been here a long, long time. I've been here many more years than I can remember. I have been here many times, almost in this same place. I have sprung up, fallen down and come back again. There was a time when everything was covered with ice. But I was here waiting. And then, when the climate became acceptable, I sprang up again. Then I fell over, but there was a part of me which came once more. So I just am. Once, I thought it

would be nice if only my species were here, all of us together; what this would be like. But then someone came and said, no, this cannot be, because there would be no room, not enough food. You'd have to stop growing and you'd all become sick. So then I did not think that anymore.

When I was imagining the spirits of the forest I saw them with little hooves on their feet. What do you think they look like?

You mean the fauns, and the wood nymphs? Some of them talk a lot and make many sounds, others don't like to speak. There are so many of them. They're all about peeping and running, so you might say we actually have a very busy location here. They are adapted to this terrain. They have feet that work well to climb hills. But I think they do not need to climb. They can place themselves wherever they need to be, from the top to the bottom [of this forest].

Do you know the redwood who calls himself Bushwark?

There are so many friends in this forest, I do not know that name. Oh yes, we know who you mean. He is bitter because he is in a spot where everyone can touch him. Do you see how I am more complete in my structure? I don't have so many nicks and scratches as he does, so I like this better.

Why do some trees seem to be not so happy?

We are many different spirits with many different points of view but we agree on most things because we all hold hands under the earth and feel many of the same things. But some are scouts or missionaries, and they wish to propel their thoughts further out. Through the contact that Bushwark has had with so many humans, he has felt much empathy with them and has come to think about them, and talk with them. He is more worldly-wise you might say, while I am content to play with the little creatures, the dancing elves that come by, and be by myself in my rituals, and my practice of growth and beingness.

Tree, we want to know the truth, no beating around the bush. Is there competition among trees, such as, who's the biggest?

This is not the same for us as it is for you. We each have our space. We are planted where we are and we depend upon one another for warmth and love and we hope that the trees and plants in other parts of the forest [the world] are as happy as we are and are getting what they need. This environment has come about over millions of years and we are perfectly adapted to it.

We come from a time when everything was bigger: men and animals, and so we are reminders of such times.

Have you ever seen a cat?

Certainly foxes, and wolves. I know what you mean about house cats because I know your minds. I see your pictures and then I know. Now most of the animals stay away from you humans.

What do you want to tell people of the world?

Yes, it is about time that people of the world heard what we have to say for we ourselves cannot tell them so clearly. We need helpers like you, so thank you for sending our message.

If we have a message it is: be happy just to be as you are. Just as we flourish in a forest that is well-suited to our needs, so do you live in a world that is well-suited to your needs. You strive too much. You try to replace what is naturally given to you. You try to improve upon, or make everything better. You don't have to do this, but your minds are always working, working.

We feel and think on subtle levels. You do not realize that our minds are also working, yet we have the capacity to relax and be more calm in the moment. We don't worry. But you have legs which take you far. And so you ask more questions and try more things. Our legs keep us rooted in the earth where all answers are automatically given.

Do a lot of people come and talk to you as we are?

Not many. But I have had some. I have had some giant beings come. Though they look like you, they are almost as tall as I. They have not come by for a long, long time. You could not see them with your eyes. Of the humans that walk by, many look upon me and I communicate my thoughts of, "Hello! Good day." and I think I see them feeling glad, though they may not know that I have greeted them.

This conversation has been most interesting to me and I thank you for this opportunity. I wish you good luck with your book.

CHAPTER SIX
A Message
From
Mother Earth

(Channeled by the author)

*y friend, you may call me Love,* or The Loving Mother. You have asked me about the plants and forests. All of these, along with your human selves, are my children. You are born of me, and spring from me. I LIVE as do you and I hold my place within this firmament as I indulge my own longing for the higher virtues, the greater understandings. I, too, have questions to be answered, but I am happy to take this opportunity to answer those of yours that I am able.

Is there intelligence in lifeforms beyond those you under-stand to be "cognizant?" Do plants, rocks, birds, air, have intelligence? Yes, my friend, you would be frightened if you knew the scope of intelligence and that it exists in all things. But you would not recognize intelligence in all of these areas because it does not correspond to your ideas regarding that which is worth thinking about.

If you ask a plant what it fears, it cannot truly respond for fear is not within its realm of experience. If there is a purpose to plant life, beyond the physical symbiosis it shares with all life on earth, it would be nothing more than to express love in merely being. This might seem to you a dumb occupation, but then you have spoken to many of my creatures and asked them about themselves and come to understand that they need nothing except to fulfill their roles and to receive a little love while they're at it. Fortunately, they bask in love and are never in need.

Must a tree sound "like a tree" when it speaks? I don't know how a tree should sound, except perhaps not much different than the Earth herself speaking! The tree will address you according to your level, much as you might adjust your dialogue when speaking with a child, an adult, or a foreigner with limited comprehension of your language. That's not to say the tree talks down to you. More it is that all knowledge exists in the higher awareness of each soul and when you tap into it you are reaching its heart: a being of perhaps millions of years of existence. So what you will generally hear is the result of the soul's having been around a long time and seen many things! It has acquired much experience which it may impart to any who will listen.

If you experience a certain initial hesitation from your friends the trees and flowers, it is only as they adjust themselves to your auric field and learn to communicate with you. After all, you have been practicing such spirit communication now for some years. It is simply new to many of them—but not unwelcome! You have added much to their lives, giving them insights into you humans they might never have had. Moreover, your love is expressed to them which gives them hope.

You wish to know of the hierarchy of beings involved in the "social systems" of plants? There are lords who monitor large areas of the earth's growth. These are angels and their ilk, some of them being in forms which you would not recognize as "alive," were you to view them. Some are so vast and formless they are like air. Then there are abundant devas, or special spirits who are the keepers of each species; who were created at the origination point of each species. Although these spirits maintain their assignments, they may be constantly splitting off, merging and reforming as new species are required.

Yes, there are individual plant souls, or personalities. Each one is complete as are you, but as with you, there can be a complex soul structure behind the scenes, so to speak.

You asked of grass, for instance. Does each blade have a soul,

a separate life? Yes, each rooted individual has its own personality though it may be described as having a "hive soul." That is, though they are individuals, their consciousness is yet entwined with the "group" or cluster of like plant life; or even with diverse species within a specific locale. Therefore, the personality and emotions of each individual may rise and fall with that of the group, each one, in effect sublimating its individuality, or perhaps contributing its essence, to the greater group consciousness. This is not as prevalent a concept among greater trees, larger individuals. Yet a park full of conifers may experience similar group "emotions," while also possessing unique personalities.

You see, it is not so necessary for them, as it is for you, to express individuality. They are not ego bound as you are. They require no such proof of their aliveness as individual achievement provides for you. Make no mistake, your path is not wrong. You are clearly designed to express differently than plants, but you would at times find comfort in being a little more like them, which is something that comes through in many of your interviews. If only because you share a common ancestry through the earth. And so, communing with me, Mother Earth, and with my rooted babies will feel naturally pleasant for each of you.

With regard to the future of this planet, there will continue to be earth movements, erratic weather patterns, earthquakes, volcanoes, and so forth, as adjustments take place. And many will continue to predict doom. You already know that those who require—or create for themselves through expectation—such experiences will "enjoy" them, while those focused elsewhere will manifest a different experience.

I am really not all that disturbed about the havoc you humans have wrought upon my surface. It is like a case of adolescent acne. It is transient and correctable. Such is the "nature" of my work; of my larger self. You have made ugly scars upon me on a microscopic level, and you have killed my creatures in your attempts to assert your superiority, a longing created by your negating of your own larger self, and a dwelling upon the outer, or physical, small self which is all many of you perceive as reality.

What you have caused, in your clumsy efforts to own, to command, to provide yourselves always with more of what you think you do not own—and more of what you feel will make you better, or happier persons—these things I have in abundance. My surface skin is resilient. If you drink my oil, I have more to give. If you tunnel deep within my surface, I heal the wound. Through a small hiccough I right again the things you made "wrong."

Watch a colony of ants. Their endeavors are so important to them, as their little social structures they uphold; as their hierarchies of leadership they employ; as their minute grains of food they labor to forage for the community. They seem so self important as they burrow holes through my soil and my trees, and yet they are nothing but some of the tiniest of creatures.

Watch yourselves as you make your way through your day, scurrying, hurrying, worrying about all that which seems so important, so world-shatteringly important to you. Realize you are but ants, going through the same survival processes, but for your minds which add such complexity to your doings. There is truly nothing more important in your lives than eating, creating, recreating and procreating. All else is just the lemon wedge on the edge of the glass.

Abundance is all around you. *I am abundance.* And this is my gift eternally to you. Even in raped forests there is yet abundance; there is yet life. Moreover, there remains in such ruins the expectation of new growth, and as you know from your nursery interviews, there exists as much courage, determination, enthusiasm, love, optimism and joy in the fledgling growths as in any mature forest. After all, the souls inhabiting my creatures great and small are all equal.

If the exact destiny of the world, of myself and all my babies could be foretold, it would naturally take the fun out of living! Be unconcerned, for as the plants advise you, it is enough to raise your arms in loving tribute to the Sun and to the Creator with absolute faith that love shall not lead you astray.

LESLIE CABARGA is the author of more than two dozen published books on graphic design, illustration clip art and cartoon animation. He is also an illustrator, type designer, roller skater and, of course, a spirit channel.

He lives in Los Angeles with his wife and younger daughter.